Visual Reference Basics

Microsoft®
Access 97

D. Bass

Acknowledgements

Managing Editor
Jennifer Frew

Project Manager
Aegina Berg

Technical Editor
Kit Bernthal

Layout and Design
Jeffrey Kurek

Table of Contents

iii

iv

Introduction

What is a database?

A database is a collection of related information. For example, a telephone book is an example of a database; it contains related information about each person listed in it: his or her name, address, and telephone number.

A database contains records and fields. A record is a collect ion of different types of information about the same subject. In the case of the telephone book, each person (listing) is a record. A field is a category of information; in the case of the telephone book, the category "Address" is a field.

Field

Name	John Smith
Address	123 Main Street ◄——— Record
City	Willowbrook
Tel. No.	630-222-5555

One of the useful things about a database is that, unlike a telephone book, it not only stores data, it allows you to sort and organize it. You can easily find records that have common characteristics. For example, you could sort out and list all the people whose telephone number begins with 222, or even all the people who live on Main Street whose telephone number begins with 222.

What is Access?

Access is a *relational* database, A relational database utilizes two or more tables (covered in more detail on the next page), containing data arranged in rows and columns, to cross-reference and define *relationships* between the data. In contrast, a *flat-file* database is limited to a single table.

A relational database breaks the "big picture" into smaller, more manageable pieces. For example, if you were gathering information about a new product line, each type of information— product, seller, and distributor—would be stored in its own, related table, rather than in one large, all-inclusive table. This unique ability to store data is smaller, related groups gives a relational database much more efficiency, speed and flexibility in locating and report-ing information.

Elements of a Database

A *table* is a collection of data about a specific topic, such as business contacts or a book collection. The table is the basic element of the database. Tables organize data into *rows*, called *records*, and *columns*, called *fields*. Records and fields, combined, make up the table.

Each *record* (row) contains information about one item or entity and is a complete record of the item. For example, in a table titled "Books," all the information about one book is in one row.

Each *field* (column) contains information of a certain type for all records. A field consists of a name or category, such as "Publisher," and an entry, such as "Ramona Publishing." The field "Publisher" contains the title of the publisher of each book in the "Books" table.

The Database Window

In addition to tables, Access 97 has many features that enable you to manage data in meaningful ways. You can view the data from different perspectives using forms, extract data based on certain conditions using queries, analyze the data in different ways using reports, and utilize various automatic procedures, such as macros and modules.

The *database window* is where all elements of an Access database are brought together. Each time you open a database, the database window displays information about the database and each type of object it contains. All information associated with a given project is available with a few clicks of the mouse. This organizational concept allows you to work effectively and creatively by dealing with the pieces of the big picture individually.

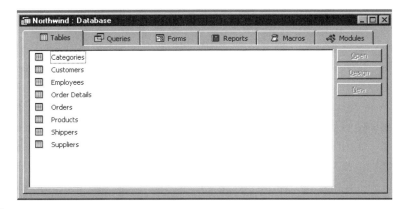

The features of the database window are as follows:

Tables   Clicking this tab displays a list of all tables in the current database. From here you can open or modify the design of an existing table, or create a new table.

Queries   Clicking this tab displays a list of all queries in the current database. A *query* is either a question about the data stored in your tables or a request to perform an action on the data. It is what enables you to break your data down into meaningful pieces. From here you can open or modify the design of an existing query, or create a new query.

Forms   Clicking this tab displays a list of all reports in the current database. A *report* is where you prepare and view or print a presentation of your data in a format of your choice. Examples of reports are sale summaries, phone lists, and mailing labels.

Macros
Modules   Clicking one of these tabs displays a list of all macros or modules in the current database. A *macro* is a written set of instructions (a small program) that automates a repetitive task. A *module* is a collection of procedures stored as a named unit.

A Note to the New Access User

Microsoft Access 97 is an extremely complex program. This guide is written for the computer user who has some familiarity with the concepts involved with creating a database—either flat file databases or relational databases. If you would like help with fundamental database concepts, the following books are available from DDC Publishing: *Learning Microsoft Office 97* and *Microsoft Access 97 Short Course.*

Create a Database Using a Wizard

The database is the starting point in Access. Office 97 provides Wizards to assist you in completing many tasks, such as creating a database, that you would otherwise have to do manually. Using a Wizard is often the simplest and fastest method of completing a task and can reduce the chance of mistakes. The Wizard walks you through a process step by step and even does a lot of the work for you.

Notes:

* See Appendix for a list and description of database templates.

1 If you just launched Access, select the **Database Wizard** option from the opening Microsoft Access dialog box and click [OK] (or press **Enter**).

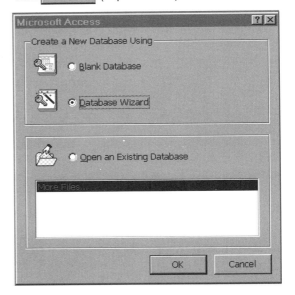

OR

If you are already in Access, select New Database... from the **File** menu (or Press **Ctrl+N**).

2 Select the Databases tab.

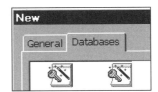

3 Double-click the icon for the desired database template.

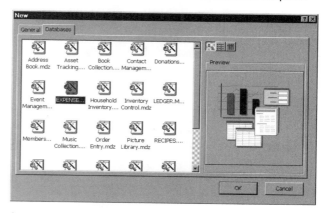

4 Select a folder in the **Save in** drop-down list box, then type a **File name** in the text box.

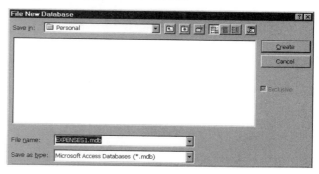

5 Click ⌐Create⌐ (or press **Alt-C** or **Enter**).

6 The Database Wizard will open and display a screen telling you what the database will store.

7 Click ⌐Next >⌐ to change the default database options.

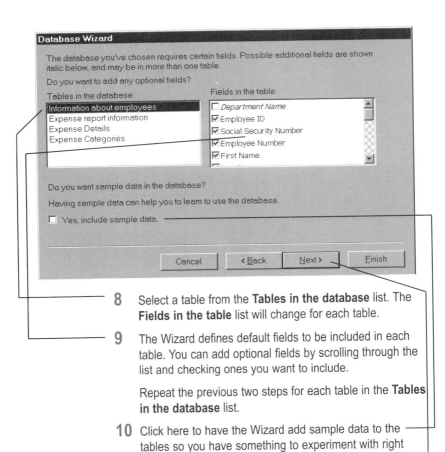

8 Select a table from the **Tables in the database** list. The **Fields in the table** list will change for each table.

9 The Wizard defines default fields to be included in each table. You can add optional fields by scrolling through the list and checking ones you want to include.

Repeat the previous two steps for each table in the **Tables in the database** list.

10 Click here to have the Wizard add sample data to the tables so you have something to experiment with right away.

11 Click **Next**.

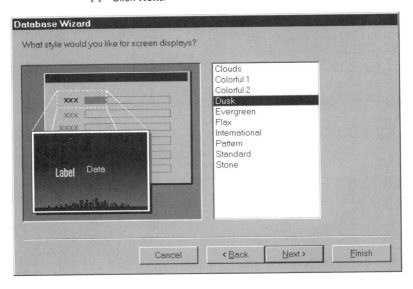

12 Select a default style for forms.

A sample is displayed in the pane on the left of the dialog box.

13 Click **Next**.

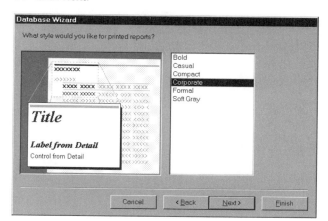

14 Select a default style for reports.

A sample is displayed in the pane on the left of the dialog box.

15 Click **Next**.

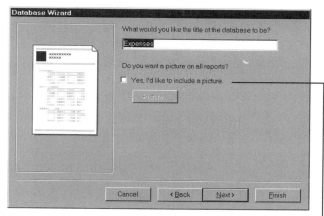

16 Type a title for the new database. This title will be displayed on the main form created by the Database Wizard.

17 Click here to include a picture such as a logo, on each report.

Notes:

• The default styles shown are called AutoFormats and can be customized. (See **Customize a Report AutoFormat**.)

5

18 Click [Picture...] to open the Insert Picture dialog box.

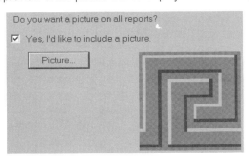

19 In the **Look in** drop-down box, select the folder where the picture is stored.

20 Select the desired picture.

21 Click **OK**.

A preview of the picture will be displayed in the dialog box:

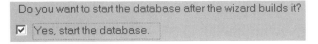

22 Click **Next**.

Do you want to start the database after the wizard builds it?

☑ Yes, start the database.

23 Check **Yes start the database**, if desired.

24 Click **Finish**.

The Database Wizard will then generate a working database application complete with tables, forms, reports, etc., all of which can be further modified and customized.

Next Section

Open a Database

Opens any database and displays the Database window.

File ➡ Open Database...   Ctrl+O

If you are already in Access

1 Select 🖻 Open Database...   Ctrl+O from the **File** menu,

OR

Click the Open Database button 🖻 on the Standard toolbar.

2 In the Open dialog box, select the folder that contains the database you wish to open from the **Look in** drop-down list.

Notes:

• Only one database can be open at a time in Access.

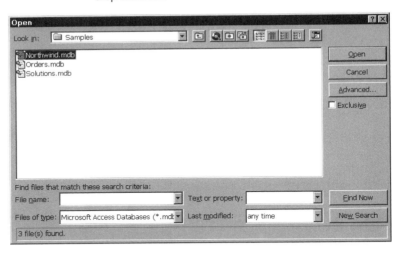

3 Double-click on the database, or select it and click Open.

If you just launched Access

1 Select the <u>O</u>pen an Existing Database option from the opening Microsoft Access dialog box.

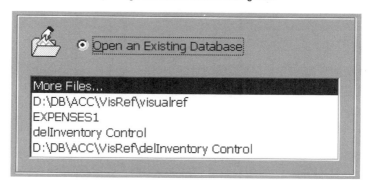

2 Double-click on a line in the list of recently opened databases.

OR

• Double-click on **More Files**.

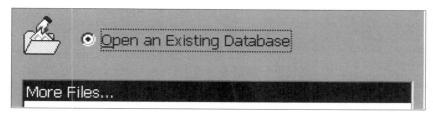

• Follow instructions in steps 2-3 of the previous subhead, "If you are already in Access".

Change Database Window Display

Database Toolbar

• To display database objects as large icons in the Database window, click the Large Icons button on the Database toolbar.

• To display database objects as small icons (as shown above), click the Small Icons button on the Database toolbar.

• To display database objects in a list, click on the List button on the Database toolbar.

• To display database objects in a list with details, click on the Details button on the Database toolbar.

OR

Right-click in the Database Window, select **View**, then **Large Icons**, **Small Icons**, **List** or **Details**:

10

Notes:

- To line up icons in the Database window without arranging them in any specific order, select **Line Up Icons** from the **View** menu or right-click in the window and select **Line Up** from the pop-up menu.

1 To tidy up the Database Window from something like this:

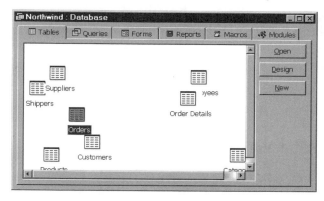

Right-click in the Database Window, select **Arrange Icons** from the pop-up menu.

Notes:

- Database objects can be arranged alphabetically, by type, by creation date, or by last modified date.

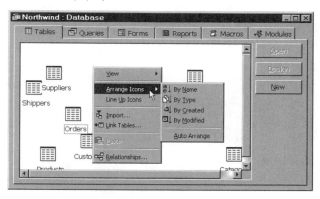

2 Select one of the following:

11

Add/Edit Relationships Between Tables

Relationships link information stored in separate tables. When you add a relationship, you inform Access that data in one table can be matched up or linked with data in another table using a field present in both tables.

Notes:

- A database is a family. Tables are family members, and relationships link them together. Some tables will be parent tables; others will be child tables. Some will be both a parent and a child. A well-designed relational database will consist of two or more tables related by one or more common fields.

Display Relationships

1 To open the Relationships window, click the Relationships button [icon] on the Database toolbar.

   Note: A database must already be open.

2 The Relationships window will open.

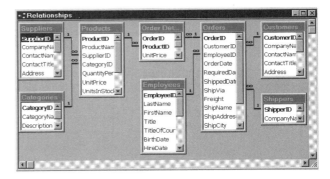

Add a Relationship

1 If the table that is to be in the relationship is not displayed in the Relationships window, click the Show Table toolbar button [icon]. If it is displayed, skip to step 4.

2 On the Tables tab in the Show Table dialog box, select each table you wish to add to the Relationships window (hold the **Ctrl** key to select multiple tables), then click [Add].

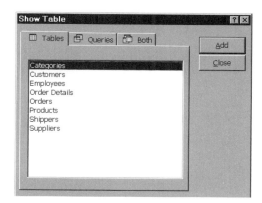

3 Click Close.

4 Drag a field name from one table to the linking field name in the related table.

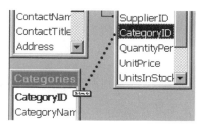

When you release the mouse button, the Relationships dialog box opens.

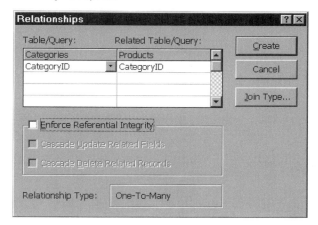

Notes:

- Use the Cascade Update Related Fields option to ensure that whenever a field value is changed, all related fields in other tables are also changed. Use the Cascade Delete Related Records option to ensure that whenever a parent record is deleted, all child records are also deleted. For example, if you delete an order for a customer, not only will the order be deleted from the Orders table, but all order items will be deleted from the Order Items table.

5 Turn on the option to enforce referential integrity if desired. You can then enable the Cascade Update Related Fields and/or Cascade Delete Related Records options.

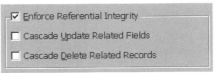

6 Click [Join Type...]; the Join Properties dialog box appears.

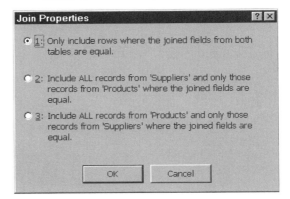

7 Select the desired Join Type, then click OK.

8 Click Create to complete the new relationship.

To Edit Existing Relationships

1 Double-click the thin line segment connecting two tables in the Relationships window to display the Relationships dialog box.

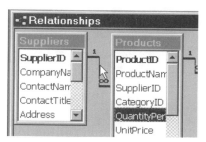

OR

Right-click the thin segment and select **Edit Relationship**.

The Relationships dialog box opens (see step 4 under Add a Relationship).

Follow steps 5-7 of Add a Relationship.

2 Keep clicking OK to save changes or Cancel to discard until you are back in the Relationships window.

3 Close the Relationships window by clicking the window close button ⊠.

Link a Table from Another Source

Data in linked tables can be viewed and usually updated, but the structures of the tables themselves cannot be changed. When you link a table, data created in another database application can be used by that application and by Access as well, eliminating the need to maintain two separate copies.

1   Open the database to which you would like to add a linked table.

2   In the Database window, select the [⊞ Tables] tab, then click [New].

3   In the New Table dialog box, double-click **Link Table**.

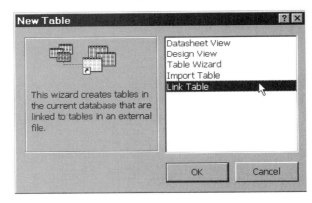

4   In the **Look In** list box, select the folder that contains the database or table you would like to link.

Link files from other than an Access database

1   Select the appropriate data type in the **Files of type** drop-down list.

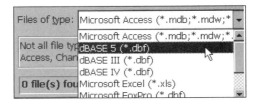

2 Select a file, then click [Link].

3 The Select Index Files dialog box opens (if appropriate for the data source).

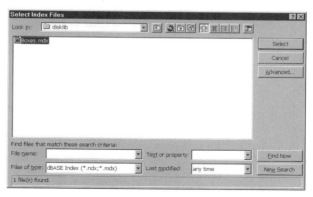

4 Double-click on an index, or select an index and click [Select].

The following message box is displayed (with the appropriate path and file name for your selection):

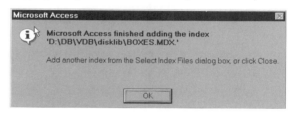

5 Click [OK].

6 Repeat steps 3-5 or click ⊠.

7 The Select Unique Record Identifier dialog box opens. Click on the item that most uniquely identifies each record in the table.

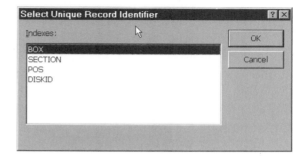

Notes:

• One field in every table should identify each record in a table as unique. This field is usually called the primary key and is also the "most unique" field in a table. Without it, linked tables may not be properly updated in queries with joins. You can also create a primary key from multiple fields if one field alone will not identify a unique record.

8   Click [OK].

A message box displays, confirming that your data source was linked.

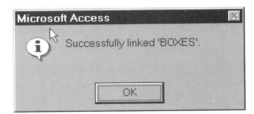

9   Click [OK].

10 Click ☒ to close the Link dialog box.

Link tables from another Access database

1   Select Microsoft Access in the Files of type drop down list.

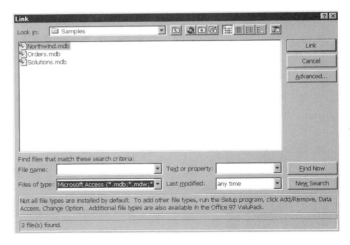

2   Select a database, then click [Link].

3   The link Tables dialog box will open.

4   Select the tables you would like to link into your database.

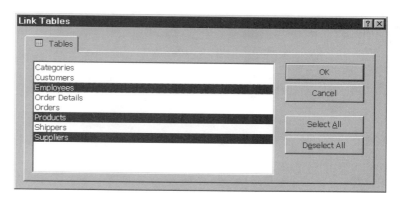

5   Click [OK] when all selections have been made.

The linked tables will display in the Database window with right-facing arrows next to the table icons. Tables linked from sources other than an Access database will have an appropriate icon identifier, such as dB (dBase) in the example shown.

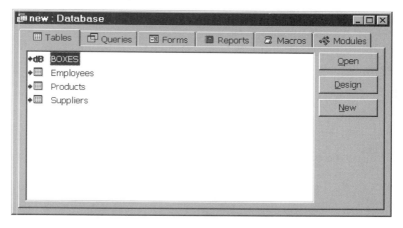

19

Create a Table Using a Wizard

Tables are the basic structural element in a database. You can create a table using a Wizard or create a table manually.

1 Open a database.

2 Click the drop-down arrow on the New Object toolbar button and select **Table**.

   Note: *The icon on the New Object toolbar button will vary depending on the last selection made from the drop-down menu.*

   OR

   Select the Tables tab in the Database window, then click New .

3 In the New Table dialog box, double-click on Table Wizard.

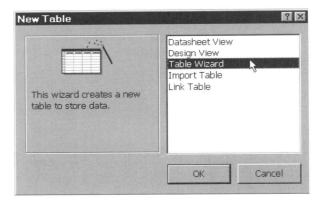

4 The Table Wizard opens. Select one of the Sample Tables on which to model your new table. The list of Sample Fields changes depending on the selected Sample Table.

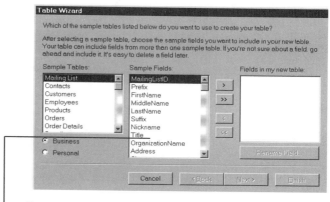

5 Select each field that you want in your new table, then click > . The field will be copied to the **Fields in my new table** list.

6 To rename a field added to the **Fields in my new table** list, select it and click Rename Field... . The Rename field dialog box opens. Type the new field name, then click OK .

7 After selecting and renaming all the fields you'd like in your new table, click Next > . In this step of the Table Wizard, you need to name the new table and decide if you want the Wizard to set the primary key or not.

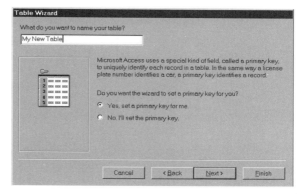

21

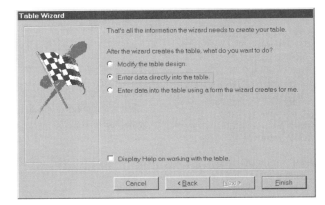
Click Next> to continue.

Note: These instructions assume that this table will be the first added to a new database. If you are adding a table to a database that already has at least one table, 5 additional dialog boxes will be displayed allowing you to define relationships between the new and existing tables (see Add/Edit Relationships).

8 The final step in the Table Wizard allows you to choose what happens next.

Make your selection, then click Finish. If you need to change something, click <Back, or click Cancel to discard everything.

Next Section

Add a Field to a Table

Increase the size of a table by adding a category of information to each record.

Notes:

- When you add new fields to a table, they are not automatically added to forms or reports. You must add them manually.

1 Open a database (See **Open a Database**) and select the ⊞ Tables tab in the Database window.

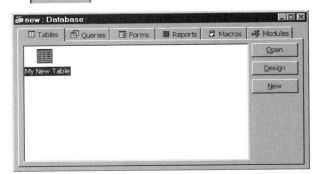

2 Select the table to which you would like to add a field, then click Design .

Design view for the table opens:

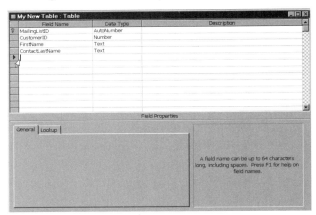

3 Click in the first blank row, then type in a new field name in the **Field Name** column.

4   Press **Enter**, or Tab to the **Data Type** column and select from the drop-down list of data types (Text is the default).

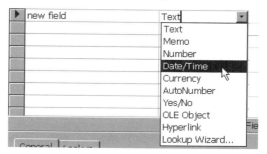

5   Press **Enter**, or Tab to the **Description** column and type a description for this field, if desired. Note this message in the bottom right of the Field Properties pane:

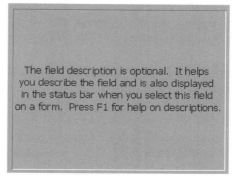

The field description is optional. It helps you describe the field and is also displayed in the status bar when you select this field on a form. Press F1 for help on descriptions.

6   Press F6 to switch to the **Field Properties** pane or click on the General tab at the bottom of the Design view window. Set other options as desired.

7   Save the table design by clicking the Save button 💾 on the toolbar.

Move a Field in a Table

Although it makes no difference to Access where fields are located in a table, it is much easier for you to work with them when they are organized in a logical order.

Notes:

- Moving a field in Datasheet view does not change the structure of the table.

- You can select multiple fields by holding the Shift key and clicking the column heading or by clicking the first column heading then dragging to select additional fields.

In Datasheet View

1 With the table open in Datasheet view (see **Open a Table**), select the field(s) that are to be moved by clicking the column heading(s) or by pressing **Ctrl+Space** with the cursor in that column.

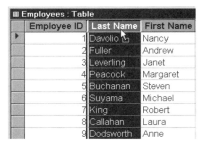

Note: *When the mouse pointer is in the column heading of a datasheet, it changes to a black down-facing arrow (see illustration above).*

2 Click the column heading of one of the selected columns and drag to the desired location.

Note: *When you click and hold the mouse on a selected column heading, the mouse pointer changes to an arrow with a transparent rectangle under it (see illustration above). This indicates that the selected column will be moved.*

The column will not move until you release the mouse button, but as you drag the mouse past a column border, a dark line appears down the column border. This line indicates where the column would be moved to if you released the mouse button (see next illustration).

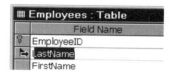

In Design View

1 With a table open in Design view, select the field(s) that are to be moved by clicking the record selector next to the field name or by pressing **Shift-Space**.

Note: *When the mouse pointer is on the record selector of a datasheet, it changes to a black right-facing arrow (see illustration above).*

2 Click the record selector of one of the selected rows and drag it to its new position. Again, the record will not move until you release the mouse button, but as you drag the mouse past a record border, a dark line will appear across the record border. This line indicates where the record would be moved to if you released the mouse button.

⊞ Employees : Table
Field Name
🔑 EmployeeID
▶ LastName
FirstName
Title
TitleOfCourtesy
BirthDate

Note: *The mouse pointer changes again when you drag the record selector of a selected row (see illustration above).*

3 Click the Save button 🖫 on the toolbar.

Delete a Field from a Table

When a field is deleted from a table, all the data in that field goes with it. Be absolutely sure you won't need the data before deleting any fields.

Edit → Delete Column

In Datasheet View

1 With the table open in Datasheet view (see **Open a Table**), select the field(s) that are to be deleted by clicking the column heading(s) or by pressing **Ctrl+Space** with the cursor in that column.

Employees : Table		
Employee ID	Last Name	First Name
1	Davolio	Nancy
2	Fuller	Andrew
3	Leverling	Janet
4	Peacock	Margaret
5	Buchanan	Steven
6	Suyama	Michael
7	King	Robert
8	Callahan	Laura
9	Dodsworth	Anne

Note: *When the mouse pointer is in the column heading of a datasheet, it changes to a black down-facing arrow (see illustration above).*

2 Right-click and select **Delete Column** from the pop-up menu.

3 If you are sure, click 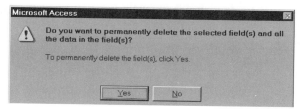 in the warning box that opens.

In Design View

1 With the table open in Design view, select the field(s) that are to be deleted by clicking the record selector next to the field name or by pressing **Shift+Space**.

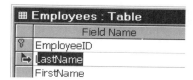

Note: *When the mouse pointer is on the record selector of a datasheet, it changes to a black right-facing arrow (see illustration above).*

2 Press the Delete key, then click 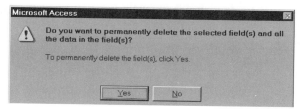 in response to:

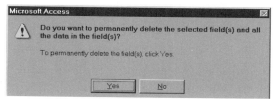

3 Click the Save button 🖫 on the toolbar.

Open a Table

Tables can be opened in two views: Datasheet view and Design view. Datasheet view displays the data stored in the table, while Design view displays the table's design or definition.

1   First, open a database (see **Open a Database**).

2   Select the ▦ Tables tab.

3   Select the table to open.

Datasheet View

Press **Enter**.

Design View

Click Design .

Next Section

Add a Validation Rule to a Field

Use a Validation Rule when you want only those entries that meet a specific criterion, such as a date range.

Notes:

- When data is entered into a field with a validation rule, it is compared to the rule for conformity. If the data does not conform to the rule, a message is displayed informing the user that an error has been made. The entry will not be accepted until the error is corrected.

- Certain data types cannot be validated and a Validation Rule field will not be present.

Notes:

- If you are familiar with expressions, you can type one into the Validation Rule field directly without using the Expression Builder.

1 In Table Design view, select the field to which a validation rule will be added.

2 Click in the Validation Rule field in the Field Properties pane at the bottom of the Design view window.

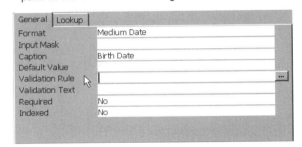

3 Click the Expression Builder button ⟨...⟩ to the right of the Validation Rule field to open the Expression Builder dialog box.

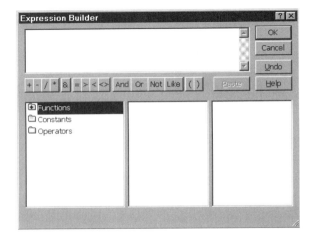

4 Type/build an expression against which entered values will be validated.

5 Click [OK].

6 Select the Validation Text field and type the text to be displayed when an invalid value is entered.

Notes:

Notes:

• Validation rules can be set for records and controls. For tables created with programs other than Access, Validation Rules can only be set for controls.

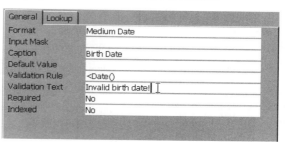

General	Lookup	
Format	Medium Date	
Input Mask		
Caption	Birth Date	
Default Value		
Validation Rule	<Date()	
Validation Text	Invalid birth date!	
Required	No	
Indexed	No	

7 Repeat steps 1-6 to add Validation Rules to other fields.

8 Click the Save button 🖫 on the toolbar.

33

Create a Primary Key

A primary key identifies one or more fields in a table that will hold unique data. No two records can have the same entry in the Primary Key field(s); Access will not allow it.

1 Open a database.

2 Select the **⊞ Tables** tab in the Database window.

3 Select the table to which you want to add a primary key and open it in Design view.

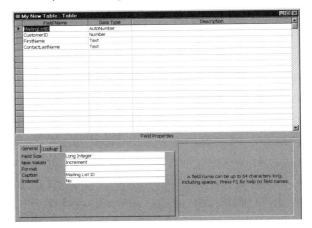

4 For a single-field primary key, click the record selector next to the field name.

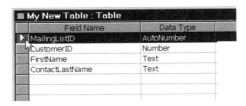

OR

For a multiple-field primary key, hold the **Ctrl** key down and click the record selector next to the fields to be included in the key.

- If the fields to be included in a multiple-field primary key are contiguous, you can click and drag the record selector from the first field to the last one to select them.

5 With the field(s) selected, click the Primary Key button on the toolbar 🔑 .

A key icon will appear in the record selector for the field(s) in the primary key 🔑▶ .

6 Click the Save button 🖫 on the toolbar.

Add an Index

Like a card catalog in a library, an index will help Access find and sort records very quickly.

1 Open a table in Design view.

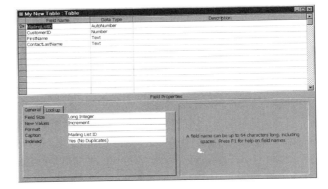

2 Click on a field to be indexed.

From the Field Properties Pane:

1 Click the Indexed field on the General tab.

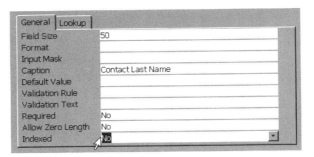

36

2 Open the drop-down list for the Indexed field and select either **Yes (Duplicates OK)** or **Yes (No Duplicates)**.

From the Toolbar:

1 Click the Indexes toolbar button [icon].

2 In the Indexes window, type a name for the new index on a blank line in the **Index Name** column.

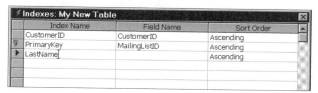

3 Tab to (or click) the **Field Name** column and select the field to be indexed from the drop-down list.

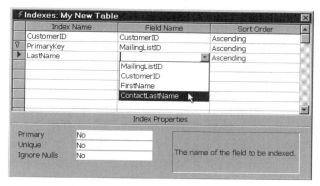

4 Choose Ascending or Descending from the drop-down list in the **Sort Order** column.

5 Select desired options in the Index Properties pane of the Indexes window.

6 Click [X] to return to the Design view window.

7 Click the Save button [icon] on the toolbar.

Sort/Filter Records in Datasheet View

Tables can be sorted by any field in either ascending or descending order. You can use filters to display a subset of desired records without using a query.

Records ➡ Sort

Notes:

- To sort more than one column at a time, select all columns to be sorted. Click the column heading(s), then use one of the methods described here. Columns must be adjacent, and they will be sorted from left to right.

- Fields with a data type of Memo, Hyperlink or OLE Object cannot be sorted.

Sort Records

1   Open a table.

2   Click anywhere in the column on which you would like to sort.

3   Click the Ascending Order **A↓** or Descending Order button **Z↓** on the toolbar.

Filter by Selection

1   Click in a field which contains the criterion by which you would like to filter. The content of the current field becomes the filter criterion.

2   Click the Filter by Selection button on the toolbar.

   Note: Three indicators let you know when a filter is applied to the current data set:

   1   FLTR appears in the status bar

   FLTR .

   2   The Apply/Remove Filter toolbar button is depressed .

   3   The Word *(Filtered)* appears next to the record navigation buttons ▶ ▶I ▶* of 24 (Filtered) .

Filter by Form

1   Click the Filter by Form button on the toolbar.

2   A window will open with one blank record. The bottom of the window displays a **Look for** tab and an **Or** tab. Enter criteria for one or more fields by using either the drop-down list boxes or by typing in an expression.

Notes:

- To improve the speed of a filter, use indexed fields. If you often need to filter on a nonindexed field, consider indexing it (see **Add an Index**).

Order ID	Product	Unit Price	Quantity	Discount
	Boston Crab Meat	Is Not Null	>30	<0.1

Look for / Or /

3   Enter additional criteria by clicking on the **Or** tab at the bottom of the window. this displays another blank record and adds another **Or** tab at the bottom.

4   Click the Apply Filter button ▼ on the toolbar.

Remove a Filter

Click the Remove Filter button ▼ on the toolbar.

Create a Crosstab Query Using a Wizard

Use a crosstab query to summarize data and group it both in rows and in columns. For instance, if you wanted to know how many orders you filled for customers in each state grouped by product, you could use a crosstab query to display each state in a different column and a different product in each row, with a count for each.

Notes:

- Access can also create a PivotTable which is very similar to a crosstab. See on-line help on PivotTable for more information.

1 Open a database.

2 Click the drop-down arrow next to the New Object button on the Database toolbar and select Query.

   OR

   - Select the | 🗐 Queries | tab in the Database window.
   - Click | New |.

3 Double-click Crosstab Query Wizard in the New Query dialog box.

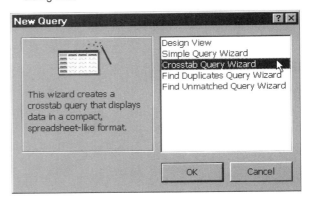

Notes:

- When selecting a record source for a crosstab query you can choose from a list of tables or queries, or both listed together.

4 Choose whether you want to display Tables, Queries, or both as possible record sources for the crosstab.

5 Select a record source from the list and double-click.

6 Select up to three fields to use as row headings and add them to the Selected Fields list by double-clicking them or by selecting each field in the Available Fields list, then clicking ▷ for each field.

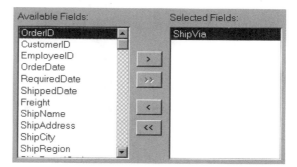

7 Double-click on a field to use for column headings.

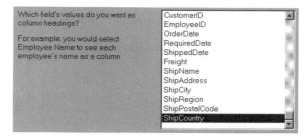

Notes:

• The Sample window changes to reflect your choices during each step of the crosstab wizard.

8 Choose a field from which to calculate a value for the column/row intersections of the crosstab. Access fills in the required expression (not shown) based on your selection of field and function. In the example shown below, the crosstab result will display a count of orders shipped to each country, grouped by the ShipVia field (see step 6).

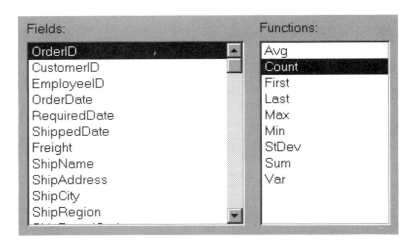

9 Click [Next >].

10 Type a name for the new crosstab.

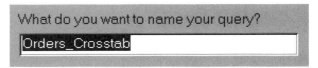

11 Choose whether you want to further modify the crosstab or view it.

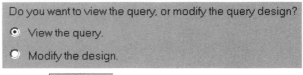

12 Click [Finish].

13 Click the Save button 🖫 on the toolbar.

Next Section

Create a Find Duplicates Query Using a Wizard

A Find Duplicates query can help you keep your tables clean by pointing out duplicate values. You can also use it to determine things like which customers have the same zip code or live in the same city.

1 Open a database.

2 Select the [🗃 Queries] tab in the Database window.

3 Click [New].

4 Double-click Find Duplicates Query Wizard in the New Query dialog box.

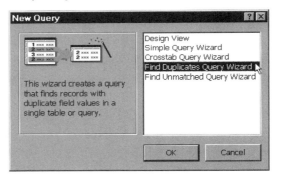

5 Choose whether you want to display Tables, Queries, or both as possible record sources in which to find duplicates.

6   Select a record source from the list and double-click it.

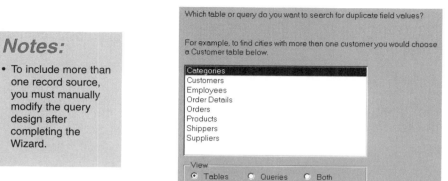

7   Select the field(s) you want to query for duplicates and click > to add them to the **Duplicate-value fields** list. To add all fields at once, click >> .

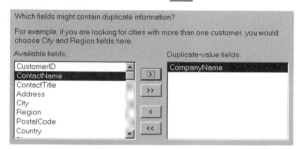

8   Click Next >.

9   Select additional fields to display in the query result and add them to the **Additional query fields** list.

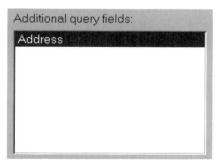

10 Click Next >.

45

11 Type a name for the new query.

What do you want to name your query?

Find duplicates for Customers

12 Choose whether you want to further modify the query or view it.

Do you want to view the query results, or modify the query design?

◉ View the results.

○ Modify the design.

13 Click Finish .

14 Click the Save button 💾 on the toolbar.

Next Section

Create a Find Unmatched Query Using a Wizard

Use a Find Unmatched query to produce a list of records from one table that do not have related records in another table.

1 Open a database.

2 Select the ⊞ Queries tab in the Database window.

3 Click New .

4 Double-click Find Unmatched Query Wizard in the New Query dialog box.

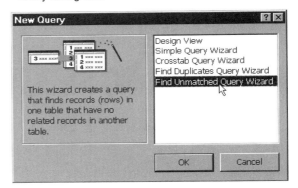

5 Choose whether you want to display Tables, Queries, or both as possible record sources in which to find duplicates.

6 Double-click a record source in the list or select it and click Next> .

48

7 Double-click the table you'd like to check for the presence of related records.

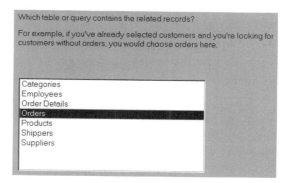

8 If it is not already selected by default, select a matching field in each table, then click <=> .

Note: *The matching fields can have different names but must have the same data type. For example, you could have a CustomerID field in one table, but in the other table it might be called CustID.*

Matching fields will be displayed below the table lists.

9 Click Next > .

10 Select fields in the Available fields list and click > to add them to the Selected fields list. To add all fields at once, click >> . These fields will appear in the query results.

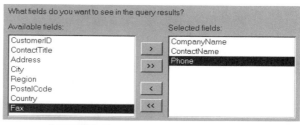

11 Click Next > .

12 Type a name for your new query.

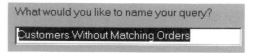

49

13 Choose whether you want to further modify the query or view it.

Do you want to view the query results, or modify the query design?

- ⦿ View the results.
- ⦿ Modify the design.

14 Click [Finish].

15 Click the Save button 💾 on the toolbar.

Next Section

Add a Table to a Query

Add a related table to expand a query.

Add a Table

1 Open a Query in Design view.

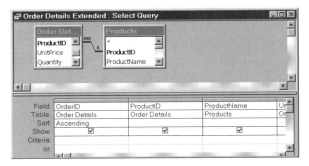

2 Click the Show Table button on the Query Design toolbar ▣ .

OR

Right-click anywhere on the Query and select **Show Table** from the pop-up menu.

3 Select one or more tables in the Show Table dialog box, then click [Add].

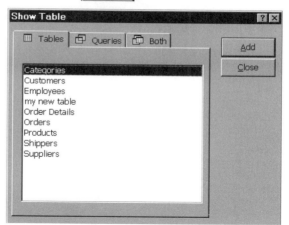

Notes:

• If relationships are already defined for the table(s), they will be inherited in the query design when you add them. If not, you will have to manually join them for the query (see **Join Tables in a Query**).

Note: Hold the Ctrl key and click to select multiple tables.

4 Click Close [X] when all tables have been added.

Delete a Table

1 Click on the table to be deleted in Design view of the query.

2 Press the **Delete** key.

Join Tables in a Query

A join matches records from one table with records in another table based on a common field. For example, a Customer table can be joined with an Orders table where the orders are matched (related) to a particular customer based on the value of a common field such as a Customer ID field.

Notes:

- If relationships (joins) have already been defined among tables in a database (which we recommend), they will be inherited when the tables are added to a query. Nothing more needs to be done in this case. However, if you did not define relationships among tables, you will have to do so after adding the tables.

1 Add one or more tables to a query (see **Add a Table to a Query**) in Design view.

2 Select a field in one table and drag it to a related field in another table.

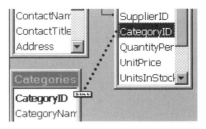

The data types must match, but the field names do not have to be the same.

A line will be drawn connecting the two fields .

Modify Join Properties

1 Open a query in Design view.

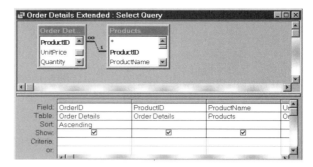

2 Double-click the thin line connecting the joined tables.

OR

54

Right-click the thin line and select **Join Properties** from the pop-up menu.

3 Select one of the options in the Join Properties dialog box.

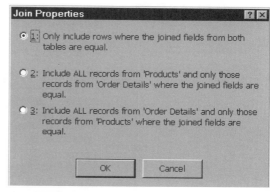

4 Click   OK   .

5 Click the Save button 💾 on the toolbar.

Add a Field to a Query

Set the criteria for the questions you want to ask your database.

1 Open a query in Design view.

2 Select a field in the table list and drag it to a blank column in the QBE grid at the bottom of the query design window.

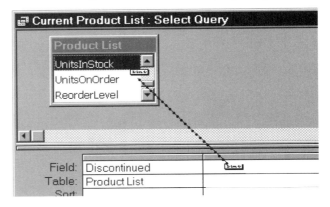

OR

Click the Field drop-down list in a blank column in the QBE grid, then select the desired field.

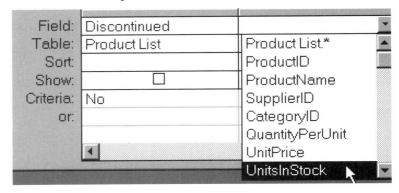

Note: *When you add a field to the QBE grid, it will be included in the query result by default. To change this, deselect the Show checkbox. However, remember to include a criterion for this field if you do not show it in the query result. Otherwise, the field will add nothing to the functionality of the query. Notice in the following illustration that although the Show checkbox for the Discontinued field is not checked, a criterion of No has been entered.*

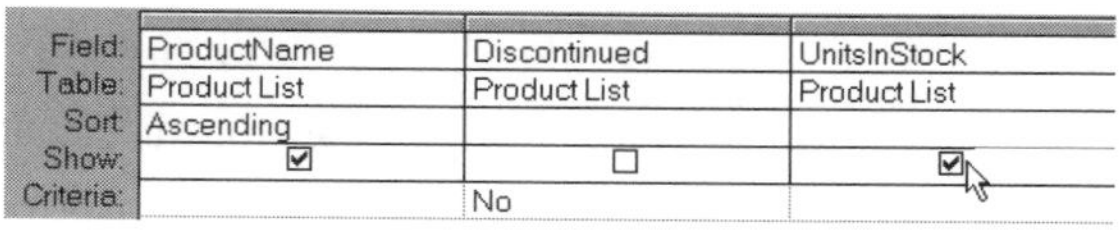

Field:	ProductName	Discontinued	UnitsInStock
Table:	Product List	Product List	Product List
Sort:	Ascending		
Show:	☑	☐	☑
Criteria:		No	

3 Click the Save button 🖫 on the toolbar.

Modify a Query to Select Unique Values

Selecting unique values is a way of eliminating duplicates in a query result.

Notes:

- Duplicate values exist when one record has the same value in the same field as another record in the same table. While this would be impossible for values in the key field(s), it is quite possible for any of the other fields in the table.

1 Open a query in Design view.

2 Click the properties button on the Query Design toolbar [icon].

Based on Fields in QBE Grid

In the Query Properties dialog box,

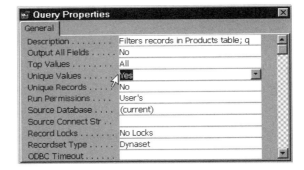

select Yes from the Unique Values drop-down list.

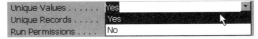

Note: *Selecting Yes in the Unique Values field automatically sets the Unique Records field to No. Only one of these properties can be set to Yes; they are mutually exclusive.*

Based on Fields in Underlying Tables

In the Query Properties dialog box,

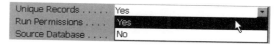

select Yes from the Unique Records drop-down list.

Note: *Selecting Yes in the Unique Records field automatically sets the Unique Values field to No.*

Change the Sort Order of a Query

A sort order is a type of filter and is saved when the form is saved.

1   Open a query in Design view.

2   In the QBE grid, click in the Sort cell for the field by which you want to sort.

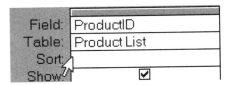

- Arrange the fields in the QBE grid from left to right in order of sort priority if sorting by more than one field. For example, to sort query results that display a list of names, make the leftmost field the LastName field, the next field FirstName, etc., so that all the same last names will sort together as well as all the same LastName/FirstName combinations.

3   Double-click to cycle through Ascending, Descending, or (not sorted).

OR

Select Ascending, Descending, or (not sorted) from the drop-down list.

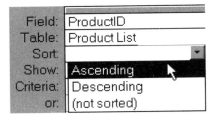

Next Section

Create a Crosstab Query

Instead of using a Wizard, you can create a crosstab query (or any other type of query) from scratch.

1 Open a database.

2 Click the drop-down arrow next to the New Object button ![icon] ▼ and select **Query**.

   Note: *The icon on the New Object button will vary depending on the last selection made from the drop-down list.*

   OR

   • Select the ![Queries tab] tab in the Database window.
   • Click [New].

3 Double-click Design View in the New Query dialog box.

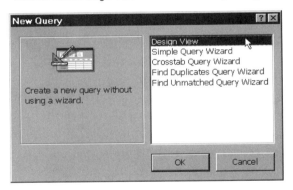

4 Add tables to the query as required and join as necessary.

5 Right-click on the background of the query window and select **Query Type**, **Crosstab Query** from the pop-up menu.

   Note: *A Total row and a Crosstab row will be inserted into the QBE grid and the Show row will disappear.*

6 Select a field for row headings from the drop-down list in the first cell in the Field row of the QBE grid.

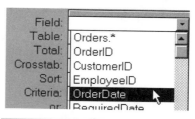

7 Select `Crosstab: Row Heading` ▼ from the drop-down list in the Crosstab cell in the same column.

8 Tab (or click) one cell to the right and select `Column Heading` ▼ from the drop-down list.

9 Move up to the Field cell in the same column and select a field for column headings.

10 Tab (or click) one cell to the right and select a field by which to calculate a value.

   *Note: You can also enter an expression; for instance, [Quantity] * [Price].*

11 Move down to the Total cell in the same column and make a selection from the drop-down list.

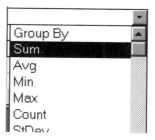

12 Move down to the Crosstab cell in the same column and select `Value` ▼ from the drop-down list.

13 Set criteria for additional fields as desired.

14 Click the Save button 💾 on the toolbar and type a name for the new query in the Save As dialog box.

15 Click `OK`.

16 Run the query by clicking the Run button ❗.

Create a Make-Table Query

One of four action queries (make-table, update, append, delete), a make-table query saves query results into a new table instead of displaying them as editable records (a dynaset).

Notes:

- A make-table query can be used to create a copy of a table to be used in another database. It can also be used to archive records before you use an update query.

1 Open a database.

2 Click the drop-down arrow next to the New Object button ![icon] ▾ and select **Query**.

   Note: The icon on the New Object button will vary depending on the last selection made from the drop-down list.

   OR

   - Select the ![Queries] tab in the Database window.
   - Click ![New].

3 Double-click Design View in the New Query dialog box.

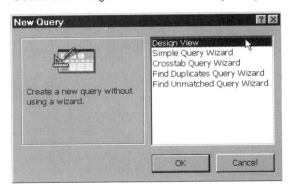

4 Add tables to the query as required and join as necessary.

5 Right-click on the background of the query window and select **Query Type**, **Make-Table Query** from the pop-up menu.

6 Enter a name for the new table in the Make Table dialog box.

7 Click <u>OK</u>.

8 Enter fields, sort order choice(s), criteria, etc., in the QBE grid.

9 Run the query by clicking the Run button ⟨ ! ⟩.

Note: *You can preview the results of the query by clicking the View button ⟨⊞ ▾⟩, but you must Run the query to create the new table.*

10 Access presents a message box telling you how many rows will be pasted into the new table.

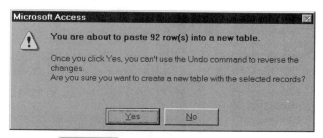

11 Click ⟨Yes⟩ to continue.

Note: *If the table exists, you'll also get a message box asking if you want to delete it. If you want to save the existing table, click No then select the table in the Database window and rename it. Switch back to the query window and run it again.*

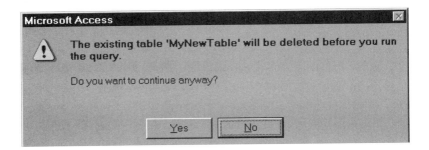

12 Click [Yes] to continue.

After you click [Yes], nothing will appear to happen
and the query design window will still be open. However, if
you select the Database window, you will have a new
table with the name you typed into the Make Table dialog
box.

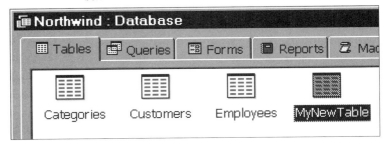

13 Click the Save button [disk icon] on the toolbar.

14 Name your new query in the Save As dialog box.

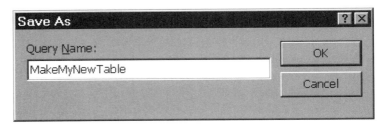

15 Click [OK].

66

Next Section

Create an Update Query

An update query changes values in existing records. This is very useful when you need to make the same change to all or a group of records.

1 Open a database.

2 Click the drop-down arrow next to the New Object button on [icon] ▼ and select **Query**.

   Note: The icon on the New Object toolbar will vary depending on the last selection made from the drop-down list.

   OR

   - Select the [icon] Queries tab in the Database window.
   - Click [New] .

3 Double-click Design View in the New Query dialog box.

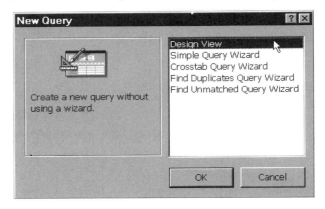

4 Add tables to the query as required and join as necessary.

5 Right-click on the background of the query window and select **Query Type**, **Update Query** from the pop-up menu.

6 Enter one or more fields to be updated in the QBE grid.

- You can limit the records that get updated by specifying criteria in the Criteria cell. For example, the query shown updates the contents of the Region field to "int'l" if it is currently blank ("Is Null").

7 Enter an expression in the Update To cell for each field to be updated 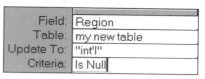.

Field:	Region
Table:	my new table
Update To:	"int'l"
Criteria:	Is Null

8 Run the query by clicking the Run button ▐ .

9 Access presents a message box telling you how many rows will be updated in the table.

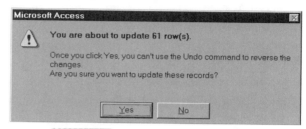

10 Click _Yes_ to continue.

Note: *After you click* _Yes_, *nothing will appear to happen and the query design window will still be open. However, if you open the updated table, the changes will have been made.*

11 Click the Save button 🖫 on the toolbar.

12 Name your new query in the Save As dialog box.

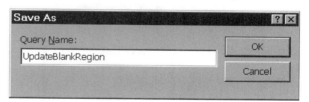

13 Click _OK_.

69

Create an Append Query

An append query is much like a make-table query, except that instead of being placed in a new table, the query results are appended to an existing table.

1   Open a database.

2   Click the drop-down arrow next to the New Object button 🗗 ▾ and select **Query**.

    Note: The icon on the New Object toolbar will vary depending on the last selection made from the drop-down list.

    OR

    • Select the 🗗 Queries tab in the Database window.
    • Click   New .

3   Double-click Design View in the New Query dialog box.

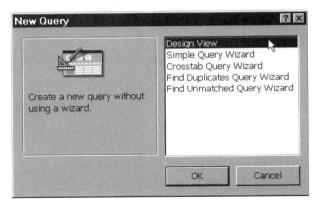

4   Add tables to the query as required and join as necessary.

5   Right-click on the background of the query window and select **Query Type**, **Append Query** from the pop-up menu.

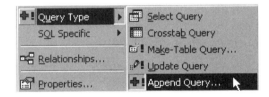

70

6 Enter (or select from the drop-down list) the **Name** of the table to which records will be appended in the Append dialog box.

Note: If you wish to append to a table in a database other than the current one, click __Another Database__, then type the name (include the drive and/or path if necessary) of the other database in the __File Name__ text box.

7 Click OK .

8 In the Field cells of the QBE grid, enter the names of the fields from which you want to copy data.

9 In the Append To: [   ] cells, enter the names of the fields to which the data will be copied.

Note: If the field names are the same, Access will fill in the Append To cells automatically.

10 If you want to append only certain records, enter the criteria in the Criteria cells.

11 Run the query by clicking the Run button [!] .

Access presents a message box telling you how many rows will be pasted into the new table.

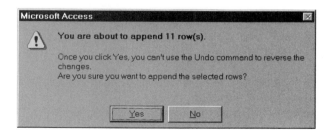

71

12 Click ![Yes] to continue.

> *Note:* *After you click* ![Yes]*, nothing will appear to happen and the query design window will still be open. However, the records will have been appended.*

13 Click the Save button ![save icon] on the toolbar.

14 Name your new query in the Save As dialog box.

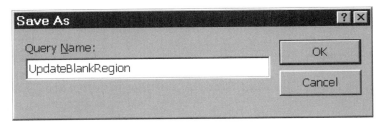

15 Click ![OK].

Next Section

Create a Delete Query

In the same way that an append query will append records to a table based on criteria, a delete query will delete them.

1   Open a database.

2   Click the drop-down arrow next to the New Object button ▦ ▾ and select **Query**.

Note: The icon on the New Object toolbar will vary depending on the last selection made from the drop-down list.

OR

- Select the ▣ Queries tab in the Database window.
- Click New .

3   Double-click Design View in the New Query dialog box.

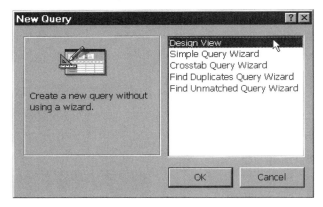

4   Add tables to the query as desired and join as necessary.

5   Right-click on the background of the query window and select **Query Type**, **Delete Query** from the pop-up menu.

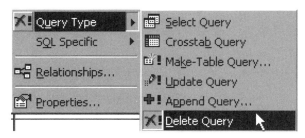

74

6 Drag the asterisk (*) from the table field list in the query window down to the QBE grid for each table from which records will be deleted.

*Note: The value in the Delete cell will contain the word From when you select a table name with the asterisk * Delete: From .*

7 Enter delete criteria in one or more of the remaining columns in the QBE grid.

Note: The value in the Delete cell will contain the word Where for delete criteria columns in the QBE grid.

8 Run the query by clicking the Run button .

9 Click the Save button on the toolbar.

10 Name your new query in the Save As dialog box.

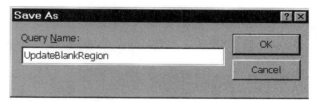

11 Click OK .

75

Create a Union Query

A union query will combine the results of two or more SQL select statements. Corresponding fields in all tables will be merged into one field in the result set. Imagine two boxes of pens in assorted colors. If you were to take all the blue ones from both boxes and put them into a third box, you will have created a union between the first two boxes.

1   Open a database.

2   Click the drop-down arrow next to the New Object button 🔲 ▾ and select **Query**.

     OR

     • Select the 🗐 Queries tab in the Database window.

     • Click 🔳 New .

3   Double-click Design View in the New Query dialog box.

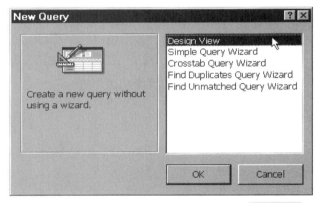

4   Close the Show Table dialog box by clicking 🔳 Close or pressing the **Esc** key.

5   Right-click in the query window and select 🔳 SQL View ▾ .

6   Click just before the semi-colon (;) and type your SELECT statement, beginning with a space.

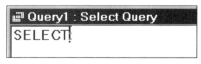

Note: *The data types of each column must match. In the following example, Table1.Field1, and Table2.Field1 are of the same data type. Table1.Field2 and Table2.Field2 are also the same data type.*

Query1 : Select Query

```
SELECT [Field1], [Field2]
FROM [Table1]

UNION SELECT [Field1], [Field2]
FROM [Table2]
```

7 Run the query by clicking the Run button ![].

8 Click the Save button 💾 on the toolbar.

9 Name your new query in the Save As dialog box.

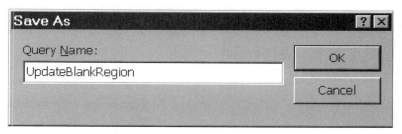

Save As

Query Name:

UpdateBlankRegion

OK

Cancel

10 Click OK .

Adjust Column Width and Row Height

The column width and row height settings are saved when you save the table.

Format ➡ Column Width... / Row Height...

Notes:

- While each column can be a different width, the row height will be the same for all rows. The row height can be set from any row.

- Double-click on the right border of a column heading to allow Access to determine the optimal column width. To resize multiple columns to the optimal width, select them first, then double-click on the right border of the column heading of any of the selected columns.

- To resize all columns to the same width, first select the entire datasheet.

Open a table, query or form in Datasheet view.

Column Width

1 Move the mouse pointer near the right border of a column heading.

2 When the pointer changes to a ⊕ , click and drag the pointer left or right to resize the column.

   Note: To resize multiple columns to the same width, select them first, then drag the right column border of any of the selected columns.

Row Height

1 Move the mouse pointer near the bottom border of a record selector.

2 When the pointer changes to a ⊕ , click and drag the pointer up or down to resize the rows.

Next Section

Navigate in Datasheet View

You can scroll through records and fields with the vertical and horizontal scroll bars.

Notes:

- Numerous navigation shortcut keys are also available. See "Use shortcut keys to navigate in Datasheet view" in on-line help.

1 Open a table, query or form in Datasheet view.

2 Resize the view so the bottom border of the datasheet is visible or maximize the window.

3 Click one of the record navigation buttons Record: I◀ ◀ [4] ▶ ▶I ▶* of 92 at the bottom of the window:

I◀	first record
◀	previous record
▶	next record
▶I	last record
▶*	insert a new record

Move to a Specific Record Number

1 Double-click the current record number in the record number box ◀ [4] .

2 Type the number of the record you want to move to.

3 Press **Enter**.

Move to a Specific Field

1 Select **Toolbars ▶** from the **View** menu.

2 Check ✔ Formatting (Datasheet) .

3 Click the Go To Field drop-down arrow CustomerID ▼ .

4 Select the desired field from the drop-down list.

80

Next Section

Create a Form Using a Wizard

While forms can be used for many purposes, one of their main functions is to display date from tables and/or queries. They can also be used as menus: you can add buttons that open other forms, print reports, or run queries.

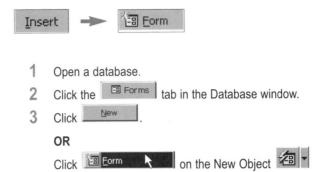

1   Open a database.

2   Click the ⊞ Forms tab in the Database window.

3   Click New.

   OR

   Click ⊞ Form on the New Object ⊞ ▾ drop-down list.

4   Click Form Wizard in the New Form dialog box.

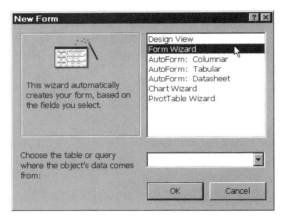

5   Select a record source from the bottom of the New Form dialog box (or type it in).

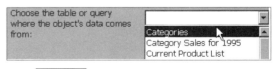

6   Click ok or press **Enter**.

7   Select fields to be added to the form and click ▸ .

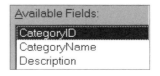

Notes:

- You can add fields from other tables or queries by selecting the name of the table/query in the drop-down list and adding the desired fields as they appear in the Available Fields list.

8 Click 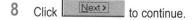 to continue.

9 Select a layout option for your new form:

Note: *As you click each option, the window to the left of*
the list displays a sample of what the form will
look like with the selected option.

10 Click [Next >].

11 Select a style for the fields and their labels from the list of
pre-defined styles.

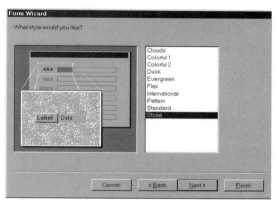

Note: *As you click each style in the list, the sample*
window changes to display your choice.

12 Click [Next >].

13 Type in a name for the new form.

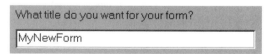

14 Choose whether to open the form or modify the form's
design.

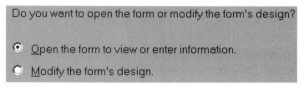

15 Click [Finish].

83

Customize a Form Using AutoFormat

AutoFormats are predefined styles that can be used to keep a consistent look among a set of forms. Existing AutoFormats can be edited and new AutoFormats can be created as desired.

Notes:

- Properties of AutoFormats can only be changed visually. There is no way to open a property sheet for an AutoFormat and make desired changes. You must add an object to a form, change its properties (or the form's properties), then create/update an AutoFormat based on the current form.

1   Open a form in Design view.

2   Change the font/color/border attributes of form elements (e.g., labels, text boxes, background, etc.) as desired.

3   Click the AutoFormat button 🖳 on the Standard toolbar.

4   Select an AutoFormat from the **Form AutoFormats** list in the AutoFormat dialog box.

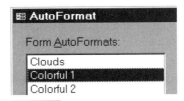

5   Click Options >> .

6   Select attributes to be saved with style.

7   Click Customize... .

    Note: If you merely want to apply a different AutoFormat to the current form, instead of clicking Customize, select the desired AutoFormat from the list and click OK *.*

8 The following dialog box displays:

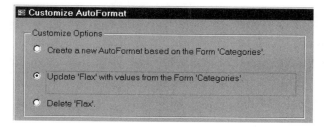

• To create a new AutoFormat, choose the first option.

• To update the selected AutoFormat, choose the second option.

• To delete the selected AutoFormat, choose the third option.

9 Click OK .

10 Click ☒.

85

Set the Record Source of a Form or Report

A form can display data from a table, query, or SQL statement. The Record Source property links a form to the data in any one of these sources.

Notes:

- If the ruler is displayed in the Design view window, you can also double-click the form selector at the top left where the horizontal ruler intersects with the vertical to select the form.

1 Open a form report in Design view.

2 Press **Ctrl-R**.

   Note: Until you click somewhere else, the form/report will be selected by default when you open it.

3 Click the Properties button 🗹 on the toolbar.

4 Click the ⬚ Data ⬚ tab from the Properties dialog box.

5 Select a record source from the drop-down list

   Record Source . . . . . . Categories ⬚ .

Next Section

Add a Subform

Displays data from another table or from another record in the same table when placed in another form. The subform is the "child" and the main form is the "master."

Open the form to which a subform will be added in Design view.

I. Locate Subform on Main form

1 Display the Toolbox (see **Toolbox Basics**).

2 Enable the Control Wizards button ⬚ in the Toolbox (see **Toolbox Basics**).

3 Click the subform/Subreport button 🖼 in the Toolbox.

4 Move the mouse pointer to the open form and drag the outline to create the approximate size for the subform. (Outline shown is for example only.)

Notes:

• After you click the Subform/Subreport button, when you move the mouse into a form in Design view, the mouse pointer changes to ⬚ .

II. Add an existing Subform

1 If the form you want to add as a subform already exists, select it from the drop-down list in the Subform/Subreport Wizard. Otherwise, go to III. Create a new Subform.

2 Click Next >

3 Type a name for the new subform.

4 Click Finish

III. Create a new Subform

If you want to create a new form to use as a subform, select
the Table/Query option.

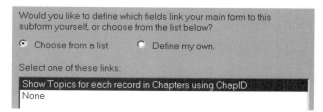

1 Click [Next >] .

2 Add fields to the Selected Fields list from the desired
tables.

3 Click [Next >] .

4 Choose a link from the list (if available).

  • Click [Next >] .

OR

  • Select ○ Define my own. .

  • Select linking fields from the **Form/report fields** and
Subform/subreport fields drop-downs.

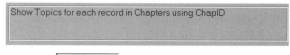

  • The link will be described in the text box below your link
specification.

> Show Topics for each record in Chapters using ChapID

  • Click [Next >] .

5   • Type a name for the new subform.

> What name would you like for your subform or subreport?
>
> New Subform

6 Click [Finish] .

89

Use Drag and Drop

1 Select the Database window.

2 Position and/or resize it so the open form is visible as well as the Database window.

3 Click the [⊞ Forms] tab in the Database window.

4 In the Database window, select the form you wish to use as a subform. Drag it to the open form in Design view.

Note: The mouse pointer will change to ⬚ while you drag a form from the Database window to the open form.

5 Place and/or resize as desired.

Next Section

Create a Pop-up Form or Dialog Box

A pop-up form remains open on top of other open forms and can be moved outside the Access desktop. If you set the Modal Property to Yes, the form becomes a dialog box. While a dialog box is open, you cannot switch to any other open windows, nor can you click anywhere outside the dialog box until you close it. You can, however, change to other running Windows applications.

Notes:

• If the ruler is displayed in the Design view window, you can also double-click the form selector at the top left where the horizontal ruler intersects with the vertical to select the form.

Notes:

• A form with the Pop Up property set to Yes has other properties that cannot be changed. It will not maximize when other windows are maximized. Also, you cannot switch to Design or Datasheet view from a pop-up form, nor will the Form view toolbar be displayed.

Notes:

• In order to use a pop-up form, you must provide a way to pop it up. One way is to add a command button using the Command Button control button 🔲 in the Toolbox with Control Wizards enabled. Follow the steps in the Command Button Wizard to create a button that opens a form (see **Add a Command button to a Form** for more information).

1 Create a new form (see **Create a Form Using a Wizard**) or open an existing form (in Design view) to be used as the pop-up form or dialog box.

2 Press **Ctrl-R**.

3 Click the Properties button 🖼 on the toolbar.

4 Click the | Other | tab in the Properties dialog box.

5 Double-click on the Pop Up drop-down list arrow

| Pop Up . . . . .Yes ▼ | to change

it to Yes.

Note: *To prevent a pop-up form from being resized, choose*

| Border Style . . . . .Thin ▼ | *(on*

the | Format | *tab of the Form properties dialog box). You may also want to choose*

| Min Max Buttons . . . . .None ▼ |. *Choosing*

| Border Style . . . . .Dialog ▼ | *will also*

prevent the form from being resized and it will override the Min Max Buttons property, removing them by default.

6 If the form is to be used as a modal dialog box, double-click on | Modal . . . . .Yes ▼ | to change it to Yes.

7 Click the Save button 💾 on the toolbar.

8 Click ✖.

Next Section

Create a Report Using a Wizard

A Report Wizard will ask you to respond to some questions, create the report, and present you with a Sample Report screen.

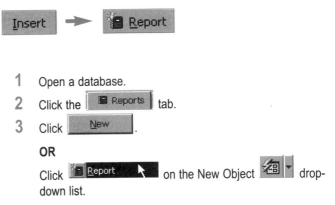

1   Open a database.

2   Click the ▣ Reports tab.

3   Click New .

    OR

    Click ▣ Report on the New Object 🖼 ▾ drop-down list.

4   Click Report Wizard in the New Report dialog box.

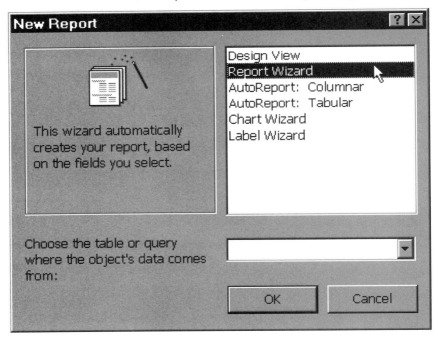

5 Select record source from the drop-down list at the bottom of the New Report dialog box (or type the name of the desired table or query).

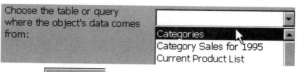

6 Click OK.

7 Select fields to be added to the report and click > (or double-click each field name).

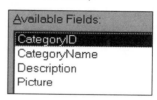

Note: *You can add fields from other tables or queries by selecting the name of the table/query in the drop-down list and adding the desired fields as they appear in the Available Fields list.*

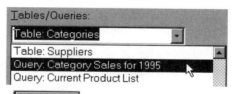

8 Click Next> to continue.

9 At this stage, the Wizard screens will vary depending on the fields you selected to be in the report.

• You may or may not be presented with screens that ask the following questions:

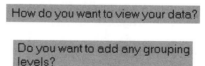

• Make your choices and click Next> to continue through each screen.

10 The steps in the Wizard converge again in the layout screen:

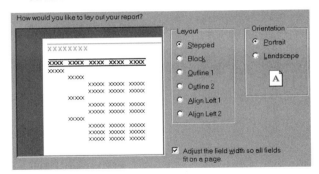

Notes:

• The available Layout options will vary depending on the fields you selected to be in the report.

• Choose Layout and Orientation options. As you choose from the Layout options provided, the Wizard displays a sample of what the selected layout looks like.

• Uncheck **Adjust the field width** if desired. It is checked by default.

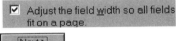

• Click [Next>].

11 Select a style from the list.

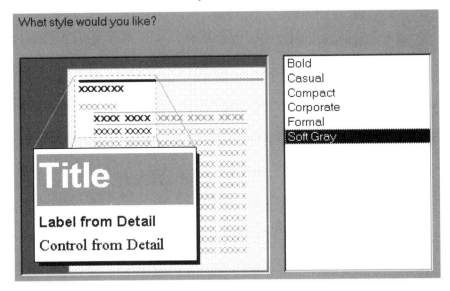

12 Click [Next >].

13 Type a name for the report:

What title do you want for your report?

MyNewReport

14 Choose an option:

Do you want to preview the report or modify the report's design?

⊙ Preview the report.

○ Modify the report's design.

15 Click [Finish].

Customize a Report Using AutoFormat

AutoFormats are predefined styles that can be used to keep a consistent look in your report.

1 Open a report in Design view.

2 Change the font/color/border attributes of form elements (e.g., labels, text boxes, background, etc.) as desired.

3 Click the AutoFormat button 📇 .

4 Select an AutoFormat from the Report AutoFormats list in the AutoFormat dialog box.

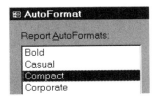

5 Click Options >> .

6 Select attributes to be saved with style.

7 Click Customize... .

Note: If you merely want to apply a different AutoFormat to the current report, instead of clicking Customize, select the desired AutoFormat from the list and click OK .

8 The following dialog box displays:

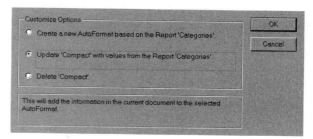

• To create a new AutoFormat, choose the first option.

• To update the selected AutoFormat, choose the second option.

• To delete the selected AutoFormat, choose the third option.

9 Click [OK].

10 Click ▣.

99

Add Report/Page Headers/Footers

Headers and footers are used to contain text that will repeat at the top or bottom of your report. You can use headers and footers to strategically place subtotal, total, and summary information.

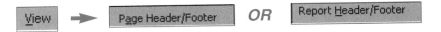

Notes:

- You can delete the header/footer bands by repeating the same steps for adding them. Use caution, however, since deleting the header/footer band deletes everything contained within them.

Notes:

- Reports can have three types of headers and footers: 1. a report header prints at the top of the first page of a report while a report footer prints at the bottom of the last page of a report; 2. a page header prints at the top of each page, and a page footer prints on the bottom of each page; 3. a detail header prints at the beginning of each detail section and a detail footer prints at the end of each detail section.

1 Open a report in Design view.

2 • Right-click on the detail band (or the report background) and select ▣ Report Header/Footer ▸ or ▢ Page Header/Footer ▸.

OR

• Select Report Header/Footer ▸ or Page Header/Footer ▸ from the **View** menu.

Note: *When you select* Page Numbers... ▸ *from the **Insert** menu, and choose one of the following options from the Page Numbers dialog box,*

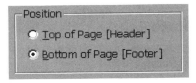

a page header/footer will be added automatically.

Next Section

Add Groups to a Report

Reports are much more readable when data is sorted and grouped. For instance, you can sort a list of companies by the country in which they are located. Each country could have its own header and all customers in the same country could be sorted by code, then by the CompanyName field.

Notes:
- You can group up to 10 levels deep.

1 Open a report in Design view.

2 Click the Sorting/Grouping button [≡ on the toolbar.

3 Select a field on which to group.

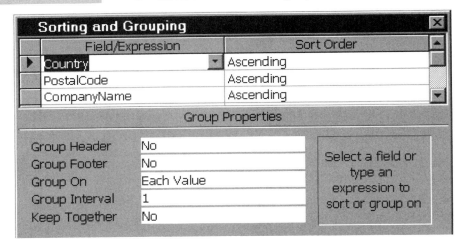

4 Select a sort order for the group (Ascending or Descending) from the drop-down list in the Sort Order column.

Notes:
- While not required for groups, effective use of a Group Header and/or Group Footer can greatly enhance the readability of a report.

5 To add a group header, change the Group Header field to Yes by double-clicking on the field, or by selecting Yes from the drop-down list.

6 To add a group footer, change the Group Footer field to Yes by double-clicking on the field, or by selecting Yes from the drop-down list.

7 Add fields and/or controls to the group header/group footer as desired.

8 To change the value that will begin a new group when the report is run, select from the drop-down list for the Group On field.

Note: 'Each Value' will always be a choice in the Group On drop-down. Other choices will vary depending on the data type of the field being grouped.

9 Type a value in the Group Interval field.

10 Select from the **Keep Together** drop-down list:

11 Click ☒.

103

Preview/Print a Report

You can preview a report before printing it to verify that everything is as you expect it to be. The preview will display the same data, formatting, and most graphics that you would see if you printed it. You can modify the report in Design view as desired and continue to preview it until you are satisfied with the results.

Notes:

- If you click the Print button, the report will be printed with all default settings.

1 Open a database.

2 Click the [Reports] tab in the Database window.

3 Click a report to preview or print.

To Preview

- Click [Preview] in the Database window.

OR

- Click the Print Preview button [🔍] on the toolbar.

To Print Immediately

- Click the Print button [🖨] on the toolbar.

OR

- Right-click on the report and select [🖨 Print... ▶].

To Print from the Print Dialog Box

1 Select 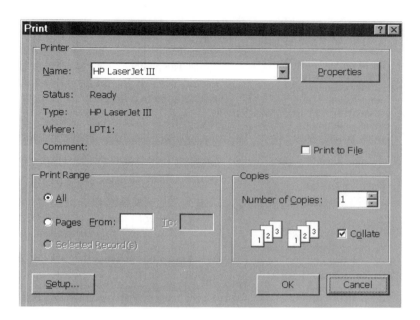 from the **File** menu.

   OR

   Press **Ctrl-P**.

Change print options such as which printer to print on, which pages you wish to print, how many copies, etc.

2 Click ▭Setup... to change Margin/Column settings, if necessary. Click ▭OK to return to the print dialog box with the settings applied or ▭Cancel to return to the print dialog box, abandoning the settings.

   Note: After changing the setup, you may want to click cancel in the Print dialog box and Preview the report again before printing (see previous section).

3 Click ▭OK to print.

Add Totals to a Report

You can add fields to calculate totals anywhere in a report, but they are most useful ina header or footer.

1 Open a report in Design view.

2 Depending on the type of total you want to print, add a Group with a Group Footer or a Page Footer or a Report Footer. (see **Add Report/Page Headers/Footers** and/or **Add Groups to a Report**).

3 Display the toolbox (if it is not already visible) by clicking the Toolbox button 🛠 on the Formatting toolbar.

4 Click the Textbox button **abl** in the Toolbox.

5 Click in the report where you want the total.

   Note: The new field will display "Unbound" with a label similar to "Text10", which is assigned by Access. This is now an unbound text box control.

6 With the textbox still selected click the Properties button 🖼 on the toolbar.

7 Select the Data tab on the Properties dialog box.

8 Click the Expression Builder button **…** next to the Control Source property.

9 Enter a formula for the calculation you want to display in the Expression Builder window.

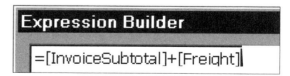

10 Click ![OK].

> Note: You can also type the formula directly into the Control Source field. The formula you enter can include names of other controls with calculations in them.

> Note: You may need to change the value of the Running Sum property, also on the Data tab, depending on the type of total you want to calculate.

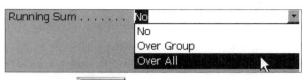

11 Select the ![Other] tab.

12 On the report, select the label that was assigned by Access.

13 Click the ![Format] tab in the Properties dialog box.

14 Type new text for the label in the Caption field

Caption . . . . Grand Total .

15 Repeat steps 4-14 to add other total fields as needed.

Create a Multiple Column Report

Multiple-column reports are useful for printing mailing labels, catalogs, directories, etc., or any data that fits nearly into rows or columns.

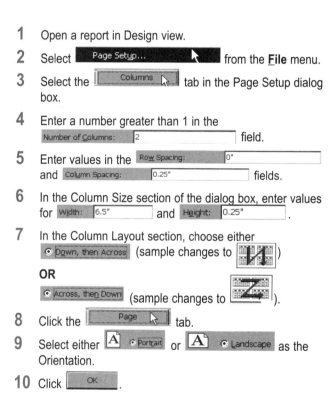

Notes:

- A report can be changed to print in multiple columns at any time after you create it. Keep in mind how many columns you want to print and allow enough space for them in the report's design.

1 Open a report in Design view.

2 Select **Page Setup...** from the **File** menu.

3 Select the **Columns** tab in the Page Setup dialog box.

4 Enter a number greater than 1 in the **Number of Columns:** `2` field.

5 Enter values in the **Row Spacing:** `0"` and **Column Spacing:** `0.25"` fields.

6 In the Column Size section of the dialog box, enter values for **Width:** `6.5"` and **Height:** `0.25"` .

7 In the Column Layout section, choose either **Down, then Across** (sample changes to)

OR

Across, then Down (sample changes to).

8 Click the **Page** tab.

9 Select either **A** Portrait or **A** Landscape as the Orientation.

10 Click **OK** .

Next Section

Add a Subreport

Combines a main report with related, parallel, or unrelated subreports.

Open the report to which a subform will be added in Design view.

I. Locate Subreport on Main Report

1 Display the Toolbox (see **Toolbox Basics**).

2 Enable Control Wizards (see **Toolbox Basics**).

3 Click the Subform/Subreport button in the Toolbox.

4 Move the mouse pointer to the open report and drag the outline to create the approximate size for the subreport. (Outline shown is for example only.)

II. Add an existing Subreport

1 If the report you want to add as a subreport already exists, select it from the drop-down list in the Subform/Subreport Wizard. Otherwise, go to III. Create a new Subreport.

2 Click Next >.

3 Type a name for the new subreport.

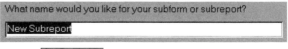

4 Click Finish.

III. Create a new Subreport

If you want to create a new report to use as a subreport, select the Table/Query option.

1 Click .

2 Add fields to the Selected Fields list from the desired tables.

3 Click [Next>].

4 Choose a link from the list (if available).

- Click [Next>].

OR

- Select ○ Define my own.

- Select linking fields from the Form/report fields and Subform/subreport fields drop-downs.

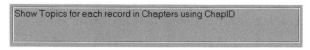

- The link will be described in the text box below your link specification.

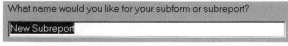

- Click [Next>].

5 Type a name for the new subreport.

What name would you like for your subform or subreport?

New Subreport

6 Click [Finish].

Drag and Drop

1 Select the Database window.

2 Position and/or resize it so the open report is visible as well as the Database window.

3 Click the [📄 Reports] tab in the Database window.

4 In the Database window, select the report you wish to use as a subreport. Drag it to the open report in Design view.

Note: The mouse pointer will change to 🖰 while you drag a report from the Database window to the open report.

5 Place and/or resize as desired.

111

Merge Data with a Microsoft Word Document

Data from an Access table (or query) can be used as the Data source for a merge in Microsoft Word. The Microsoft Word Mail Merge Wizard helps you through it.

Notes:

- You must have Microsoft Word installed for this Wizard to be available.

- This Wizard launches Microsoft Word even if it is already running.

1 Open a database.

2 Select a table or query whose data you'd like to merge with a Word document.

3 Select  from the **Office Links** submenu on the **Tools** menu:

The following dialog box displays:

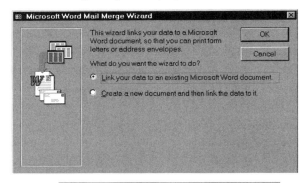

a Select ⊙ Link your data to an existing Microsoft Word document. then click OK to merge data into an existing Word document.

b The dialog box shown above opens, prompting you to select a Word document.

c Select a document (change to another drive and/or folder in the Look in drop-down box if necessary), then click Open .

OR

a Select ⊙ Create a new document and then link the data to it. then click OK to create a new document with which your data will be merged.

b Microsoft Word opens, ready to for you to create/edit your merge document.

4 Click the Mail Merge Helper button 🖼 on the Mail Merge toolbar in Microsoft Word.

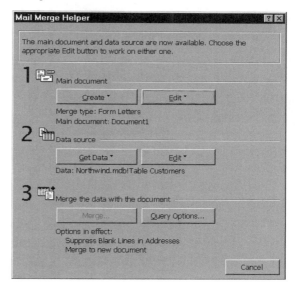

In the Mail Merge Helper dialog box that opens (shown above), verify that steps 1 and 2 have been completed. Step 1 should show a main document name Main document: Document1 and step 2 should show a data source Data: Northwind.mdb!Table Customers .

5 Click the Merge button to complete the merge.

Note: See on-line help in Microsoft Word for details on how to use the Mail Merge Helper

Create Mailing Labels Using a Wizard

The Label Wizard will create a report for any standard Avery label. Custom labels are also supported.

1 Open a database.

2 Click the **Reports** tab.

3 Click **New**.

4 Click Label Wizard in the New Report dialog box.

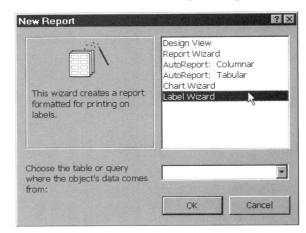

5 Select a data source from the drop-down list at the bottom of the New Report dialog (or type it in).

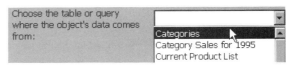

6 Click **OK**.

7 Choose a Label Type:

8 Select a Unit of Measure:

Note: The list of labels changes depending on the Label Type and Unit of Measure selected.

9   Select from the list:

OR

Click  Customize... to create a custom label.

Note: If you have already created custom labels, click ☐ Show custom label sizes to display them instead of the list of Avery labels.

10 Click Next >.

11 Make Text appearance selections from the following dialog box:

Note: The Sample text box shows a preview of your choices on the left side of the dialog box.

12 Click Next >.

13 Double-click field names in the Available fields list to add them to the Prototype label.

Add punctuation as needed to the Prototype label including line breaks, additional text etc. Although you cannot add tabs to the Prototype label, you can position fields however you want in Design view after the label report has been created. You can add fields to any available line on the Prototype label.

115

14 Click 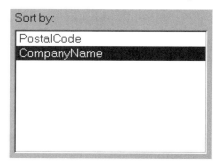 .

15 Double-click fields on which you want the mailing labels to be sorted. They will be added to the Sort by list.

16 Click 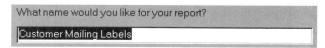 .

17 Type a name for the new report:

18 Choose whether to preview the labels or modify the design:

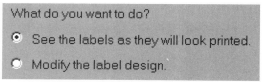

19 Click [Finish] .

Next Section

Using the Grid on Forms/Reports

The grid consists of rows of dots on the background of a form or report. It is a visual reference to help you align and place controls on forms and reports. Controls can "snap" to grid points or not, depending on your preference or need.

Notes:

- Sizing a control to the grid forces the control to resize to the closest grid point(s). This can cause the size of the control to shrink or expand depending on where the grid points are, relative to the size and location of the object being resized.

Open a form or report in Design view.

Display the Grid

Right-click a blank area of the form/report and select  from the pop-up menu.

To turn off the grid, repeat the above procedure.

Align Controls to Grid

1 Select one or more controls to align to the grid. (Hold the **Shift** key to select more than one.)

2 Select **To Grid** on the **Align** submenu of the **Format** menu:

Size Controls to Grid

1 Select one or more controls to size to the grid. (Hold the **Shift** key to select more than one.)

2 Select **To Grid** on the **Size** submenu of the **Format** menu:

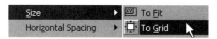

Notes:

- The Snap To Grid option can be enabled even if the grid is not displayed.

Snap To Grid

Select 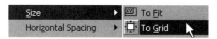 from the **Format** menu.

118

Change Grid Spacing

1 Press **Ctrl-R** to select the form/report.

2 Click the Properties button 📇 .

3 Click the | Format | tab.

4 Type a new value into
   | Grid X . . . . 24 | to change the number of dots per horizontal inch/centimeter.

5 Type a new value into
   | Grid Y . . . . 24 | to change the number of dots per vertical inch/centimeter.

119

Align/Size/Space/Layer Controls

Controls can be adjusted to enhance the look and functionality of a form or report.

Notes:

- Controls can also be selected by dragging the mouse pointer around the objects to be selected. The Selection Behavior option on the Forms/Reports tab in the Options dialog box (Tools, Options) determines how controls are selected. If Partially Enclosed is selected, you only have to drag around part of a control to select it. If Fully Enclosed is selected, you have to drag around the entire control to select it.

- You can use any combination of tools to arrange controls. Use as many as necessary in the order that makes the most sense to achieve the look you want.

Align

1 Open a form or report in Design view.

2 Select two or more controls to align. (Hold the **Shift** key to select more than one.)

3 Select from the **Format** menu.

4 Choose from following submenu:

Size

1 Select two or more controls to size. (Hold the **Shift** key to select more than one.)

2 Select  from the **Format** menu.

3 Choose from following submenu:

120

Space

1 Select two or more controls to space. (Hold the **Shift** key to select more than one.)

2 Select 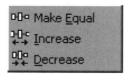 or ⬛ Vertical Spacing ⬛ from the **Format** menu.

3 Choose from following submenu:

> ᴼᴰᵒ Make **E**qual
> ᴺ**ᴵᴺ**ᶜ **I**ncrease
> ᴼᴰᵒ **D**ecrease

Layer

1 Select one or more controls to move in front of/in back of each other.

2 Select ⬛ Bring to Front ⬛ or ⬛ Send to Back ⬛ from the Format menu.

Toolbox Basics

The Toolbox contains all the controls that can be added to a form or report.

Notes:

- The Toolbox will only display in Design view of a form or report. It can be moved freely on the Windows desktop, or docked like a toolbar on any of the borders of the Access window.

Display the Toolbox

1   Open a form or report in Design view.

2   Click the Toolbox button 🪛 on the Form/Report Design toolbar.

   Note: The Toolbox button appears depressed when the Toolbox is displayed. Clicking it again removes the Toolbox from the workspace.

Enable/Disable Control Wizards

1   Open a form/report in Design view.

2   Display the Toolbox (see above).

3   Select the Control Wizards button 🪄 from the Toolbox menu.

   Note: While the Control Wizards button is depressed, a Wizard will be launched anytime you add a control. Control Wizards are disabled when the button is not depressed.

Notes:

- When a control is locked, you can add several of the same control (i.e., label, command button, text box, etc.) without clicking in the Toolbox each time. To speed things up even more, you may want to disable Control Wizards (see above) when using Control Lock.

Control Lock

1   Open a form or report in Design view.

2   Double-click a control in the Toolbox.

   Note: The mouse pointer changes to reflect the current control.

3   Press **Esc** to unlock the control.

Next Section

Add a Label to a Form/Report

A label is text that describes something on a form or report. By default, when a field (or text box) is added to a form or report, a label is added with it. The label indicates what data is being displayed (or should be entered if you are entering new data) in the field.

1 Open a form or report in Design view.

2 Display the Toolbox (if it is not already displayed), and enable the Control Wizards (see **Toolbox Basics**).

3 Click the Label button  in the Toolbox.

Note: After you click the Label button, the mouse pointer will change to ⁺A when you move it over the form or report.

4 Click and drag a rectangle the approximate size you want the label to be:

When you release the mouse button, the cursor will be inside the rectangle, waiting for you to type the text of the label:

5 Type the text for the label, then press **Enter**.

Note: If you don't type any text, the label will not be added.

124

6 The label will remain selected and will have sizing handles:

While it is selected, you can apply formatting.

7 To edit the text of a label, click on it while it is selected. If it is not selected, click once to select it, then click again to edit; this is not the same as a double-click, however.

Edit as desired:

Add a Text Box to a Form/Report

Use a text box to display a calculated value, data from a table, query or SQL statement, or to accept user input.

Notes:

- A text box is bound when it displays data from a table, query or SQL statement. Data entered into an unbound text box is not stored.

Open a form or report in Design view.

Unbound

1 Display the Toolbox and enable the Control Wizards (see Toolbox Basics).

2 Click the Text box button  in the Toolbox.

   Note: *After you click the Text box button, the mouse pointer will change to when you move it over the form or report.*

3 Click and drag a rectangle the approximate size you want the text box to be:

OR

Click once on the form or report to create a text box of the default size.

Notes:

- By default, a label is added with a text box. The label can be moved, formatted, and sized independently of the text box (see **Add a Label to a Form/Report**). You can also delete the label.

4 Open the property sheet (see **Open the Property Sheet**).

5 Click the | Other | tab.

6 Type a name for the text box into the Name field:

Name . . . . MyUnboundField

126

Bound

Note: These steps assume that the form or report has a data source.

1 Click the Field List button  on the Form Design toolbar.

A list box with the fields from the data source displays:

2 Drag a field name from the field list to the form or report.

Note: The mouse pointer will change to ▦ as soon as you begin dragging from the list box.

3 Open the property sheet (see **Open the Property Sheet**).

4 Click the ▌Other▐ tab.

5 Type a name for the text box into the Name field.

127

Add a Border to a Form/Report

Improve the look and enhance the organization of input screens or reports with lines and backgrounds.

1 Open a form or report in Design view.

2 Display the Toolbox and enable the Control Wizards (see **Toolbox Basics**).

3 Click the Rectangle button ▭ .

  Note: The mouse pointer will change to 🞡▭ when you move it over the form or report.

4 Click and drag a rectangle the approximate size you want the border to be:

OR

Click once on the form or report to create a rectangle of the default size.

5 By default, the Back Style property of a rectangle will be Transparent, which causes the rectangle to look like a border. To give a rectangle a solid appearance:

  • Open the property sheet.

  • Click the Format tab.

  • Change the Back Style property to Normal:

Back Style . . . . Normal

  • Assign other properties such as Back Color, Special Effect, Border Style, etc., as desired.

Notes:

• When the Back Style property of a rectangle is set to Normal, it can cover other controls. To correct this, select the rectangle then select **Send to back** on the **Format** menu.

Next Section

Add a Combo/List Box to a Form

Combo/List boxes are used to display a list of values. Combo boxes take up less room on a form and can be set to allow new values to be entered. List boxes are fixed in size and new values cannot be entered.

Notes:

- Since the steps to add a combo box and a list box are nearly identical, the directions and illustrations refer only to adding a combo box. To add a list box, begin by clicking the List Box button instead of the Combo Box button. Then follow all other directions.

Notes:

- By default, a label is added with a combo box. The label can be moved, formatted, and sized independently of the box. You can also delete the label.

1 Open a form in Design view.

2 Display the Toolbox and enable the Control Wizards (see **Toolbox Basics**).

Note: These instructions assume that the form has a data source.

3 Click the Combo Box button ⬚ in the Toolbox.

Note: After you click the Combo Box button, the mouse pointer will change to ⬚ when you move it over the form.

4 Click and drag a rectangle the approximate size you want the box to be:

OR

Click once on the form to create a combo box of the default size.

5 Select an option for how the combo box will get the values to display:

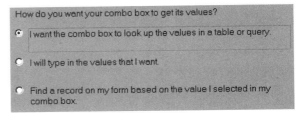

The Combo Box Wizard will display different steps depending on your selection.

6 Make a selection, then click [Next >] .

130

Look Up the Values in a Table or Query.

1 Choose whether you want to display Tables, Queries, or both as possible record sources for the values in the combo box.

2 Double-click the desired record source in the list.

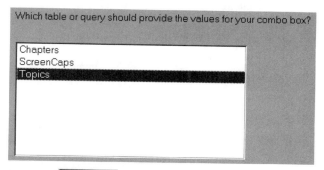

3 Click Next >.

4 Add fields from the Available Fields list to the Selected Fields list by double-clicking each field name.

To add all fields at once, click >>.

5 Adjust the width of the field(s) (now displayed in columns) by either dragging the right edge of the column heading to the desired width or double-clicking it to let Access determine the best fit:

131

Before:

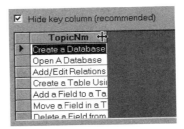

After:

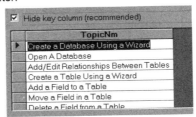

6 Click ▢ Next> .

7 Decide if you want to store the combo box choice in memory or in a field:

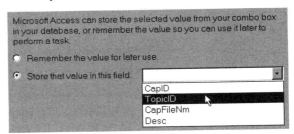

> Note: If you choose to store a value, select the field in which you would like to store the value from the drop-down list box. By default, the value stored will be the key field. You can change this on the property sheet if you need to store a field other than the key field.

8 Click ▢ Next> .

9 Type a label for the combo box:

10 Click ▢ Finish .

Typed-in Values

Notes:

- While a combo box can display more than one column of data, the value from only one of the columns will be stored when selected.

1 Enter the number of columns you want to display in the combo box:

2 Fill in the columns in the grid as if it were a datasheet. These values will be displayed in the combo box:

Col1	Col2
ID1	Topic 1
ID2	Topic 2
ID3	Topic 3

3 Adjust the column widths if desired/necessary by either dragging the right edge of the column heading to the desired width or double-clicking it to let Access determine the best fit.

4 Click [Next >].

5 Choose the field whose contents you would like to store when it is chosen in the combo box:

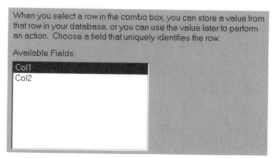

6 Click [Next >].

7 Decide if you want to store the combo box choice in memory or in a field:

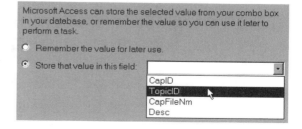

Note: *If you choose to store a value, select the field in which you would like to store the value from the drop-down list box. By default, the value stored will be the key field. You can change this on the property sheet if you need to store a field other than the key field.*

8   Click 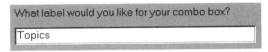 .

9   Type a label for the combo box:

What label would you like for your combo box?

Topics

10   Click 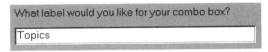 .

Find a Record Based on Combo Box Selection

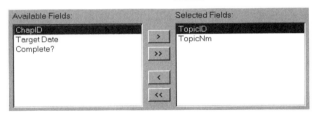

⊙ Find a record on my form based on the value I selected in my combo box.

1   Add fields from the Available Fields list to the Selected Fields list by double-clicking a field name.

To add all fields at once, click >> .

Available Fields: Selected Fields:

ChapID   TopicID
Target Date   TopicNm
Complete?

2   Adjust the width of the field(s) (now displayed in columns) by either dragging the right edge of the column heading to the desired width or double-clicking it to let Access determine the best fit.

3   Click 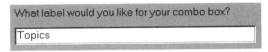 .

4   Type a label for the combo box:

What label would you like for your combo box?

Topics

5   Click 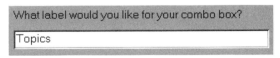 .

Next Section

Add a Command Button to a Form

Command Buttons are very versatile controls. They can be used to open or close forms, display messages, set filters, add new records, etc. They can be any size, and can display text, bitmaps, or a combination of the two.

Notes:

- Using the Command Button Wizard you can create more than 30 types of command buttons without any programming.

1 Open a form in Design view.

2 Display the Toolbox and enable the Control Wizards (see **Toolbox Basics**).

> *Note:* *These instructions assume that the form has a data source.*

3 Click the Command button 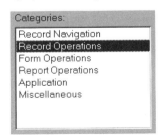.

> *Note:* *After you click the Command button, the mouse pointer will change to* ⊞ *when you move it over the form.*

4 Click once on the form to create a command button of the default size.

The following dialog box will display:

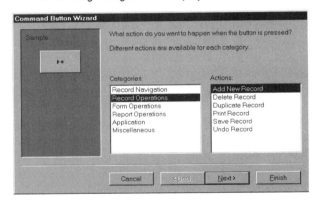

5 Select a category in the Categories list:

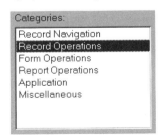

136

6 Select an action from the Actions list:

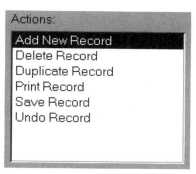

Note: *Each command has a default icon (symbol) that
will be placed on its command button unless you
specify otherwise. For example, shown below is
the Sample pane when the Add New Record
action is selected:*

7 Click [Next >] .

8 Type the text you want to display on the button in the Text
field:

OR

Select a picture from the list:

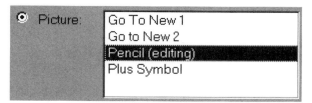

137

The Sample pane shows a preview of your selection.

Note: *For a more extensive list of pictures, click* □ Show All Pictures *. You can also select a file from another location by clicking* Browse... *.*

9 Click Next>.

10 Type a name for the command button:

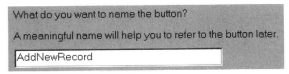

11 Click Finish.

Next Section

Move a Control

Arrange graphical objects in your forms and reports to display data, perform actions, or enhance readability.

1   Open a form or report in Design view.

2   If the control to be moved is not selected, you can click on it anywhere and drag it to the desired position in one step.

OR

If it is selected, move the pointer over one of the borders until the mouse pointer changes to a small hand:

Click and drag it to the desired position.

Use the Move Handle

When selected, each control has a move handle in the top left corner. It looks like a sizing handle but larger:

The mouse pointer changes to a pointing finger when passed over the move handle:

Click and drag the move handle to the desired position.

The outline of the control remains visible while it is being moved:

To temporarily disable Snap to Grid, hold the **Ctrl** key while moving the control.

Notes:

- You can use the **Ctrl** and **Shift** keys together to move a control on one axis without regard to the grid. However, you must press the **Ctrl** key first. In this case, you don't have to be dragging the move handle for the **Shift** key to hold the control on an axis as long as you were holding the **Ctrl** key when you began.

Use Cursor Keys

Hold the **Ctrl** key and press the cursor arrow keys to move a control in small increments.

Disable Snap to Grid

Hold the **Ctrl** key and drag to move a control without regard to the grid, even if Snap to Grid is enabled.

Open the Property Sheet

The Property Sheet is used to define and fine tune nearly all characteristics (properties) of database objects (i.e., tables, queries, fields, forms and reports). Each control on a form or report has properties as well.

Table Properties

Notes:

- Once you open the property sheet, it stays open until you close it. It will display different properties depending on what is currently selected in the window.

1 Open a database.

2 Click the [⊞ Tables] tab.

3 Right-click on a table then select [🖹 Properties] from the pop-up menu.

The following dialog box opens:

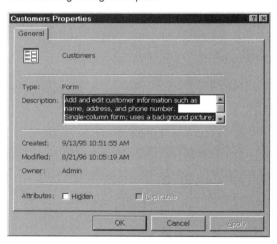

Notes:

- As shown, the name of the dialog box will be the name of the table followed by the word "Properties."

Normally, only two properties can be changed for a table:

and

Note: The Replicable checkbox may be disabled.

4 Click [OK].

142

Field Properties

Open a table in Design view.

The bottom pane of the Design view window is devoted to field properties:

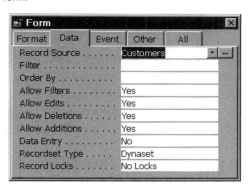

Field Properties

General	Lookup	
Field Size	5	
Format		
Input Mask	>LLLLL	
Caption	Customer ID	A field name can be up to 64 characters long, including spaces. Press F1 for help on field names.
Default Value		
Validation Rule		
Validation Text		
Required	No	
Allow Zero Length	No	
Indexed	Yes (No Duplicates)	

Note: *Certain field properties are inherited (copied) whenever that field is added from the field list to a form or report. For example, if you drag the CustomerID field from the field list to a form, the Input Mask property as shown above in table Design view will be copied to the Input Mask property for the field on the form.*

Form/Report Properties

1   Open a form or report in Design view.

2   Select the control whose properties you wish to change.

   Note: *To change the properties of the form or report, select the form or report by pressing **Ctrl-R**.*

   Right-click then select [📇 Properties] from the pop-up menu.

   The following shows the Data tab on the property sheet for a form:

🔳 Form					✕
Format	Data	Event	Other	All	
Record Source	Customers			▾	...
Filter					
Order By					
Allow Filters	Yes				
Allow Edits	Yes				
Allow Deletions	Yes				
Allow Additions	Yes				
Data Entry	No				
Recordset Type	Dynaset				
Record Locks	No Locks				

The following shows the Data tab on the property sheet for a report:

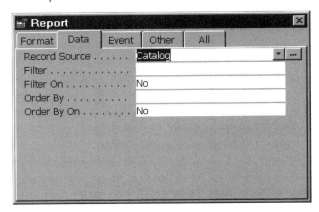

Query Properties

1 Open a query in Design view.

2 Click on the background of the query.

3 Right-click then select 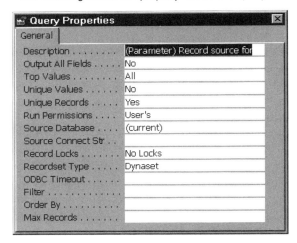 from the pop-up menu.

The following shows the property sheet for a query:

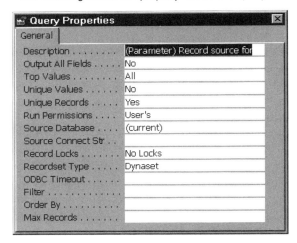

Next Section

Set Format Property

The Format property can be used to change the way data is displayed and printed. For instance, a date can be displayed and printed in any number of date formats such as 1/1/97, 1 Jan 97, January 1, 1997, etc. Numbers, dates, times and regular text can all be formatted. The actual value stored in a table is not affected by the Format property.

You can set the Format Property by opening a table in Design view and selecting the General tab of the Field Properties pane,

OR

by selecting the Format tab of the property sheet in any other view.

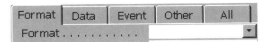

The following symbols can be used in the Format property for any data type (see "Format Property" in on-line help for more information and examples):

Symbol	Description
(space)	displays a space
"text"	displays the text between the quotation marks
!	forces left alignment
*	fill available space with character that follows
\	do not interpret the next character as a format symbol (display it as typed)
[color]	display the entry in the color specified where color is one of the following: Black, Blue, Green, Cyan, Red, Magenta, Yellow, White (Note: You must include at least one of the other formatting symbols with the [color] symbol, and the color must be surrounded by the square brackets)

146

Format a Field

1   Open a table, form, or report in Design view.

   *Note: If you open a form or report, you will also need to open the property sheet (see **Open the Property Sheet**).*

2   Select the field or control you would like to format.

3   In the Format property field, select the appropriate format from a predefined list (if provided, as described in the following sections).

   OR

   Type a custom format into the Format field using symbols and other characters (see below).

Format a Text/Memo Data Type

Text and Memo fields can have the following format symbols in addition to the ones noted on the previous page:

@   a character (or space) must be typed

&   a character is optional

<   display all characters in lowercase

>   display all character in uppercase

The Format property can have two sections: one to specify how to display data when a field has text, and another when a field is either a zero-length string ("") or NULL (blank). These sections are separated by a semi-colon. Neither is required.

To format a field to display all text in lowercase, blue letters, and include the literal text "http://www." before every entry, set the Format property to:

To use the above format and display "no entry" when a field is a zero-length string or blank, use:

147

Format a Date Data Type

Select one of the predefined date formats from the Format drop-down menu:

Medium Date	▼
General Date	6/19/94 5:34:23 PM
Long Date	Sunday, June 19, 1994
Medium Date	19-Jun-94
Short Date	6/19/94
Long Time	5:34:23 PM
Medium Time	5:34 PM
Short Time	17:34

OR

Type in a custom date format. See "Format Property — Date/Time Data Type" in on-line help for more information.

Format a Number/Currency Data Type

Select one of the predefined number formats from the Format drop-down menu:

	▼
General Number	3456.789
Currency	$3,456.79
Fixed	3456.79
Standard	3,456.79
Percent	123.00%
Scientific	3.46E+03

OR

Type in a custom number format. Custom number formats can have four sections (each separated by a semi-colon).

Format a Yes/No Data Type

Select one of the predefined Yes/No formats from the Format drop-down menu:

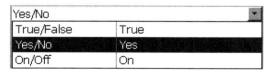

Yes/No	▼
True/False	True
Yes/No	Yes
On/Off	On

OR

Type in a custom Yes/No format. Custom Yes/No formats can have three sections (separated by semi-colons):

First   ignored; include a semi-colon as a placeholder

Second text to display instead of "True," "Yes," or "On" (text must be surrounded by double-quotes)

Third   text to display instead of "False," "No," or "Off" (text must be surrounded by double-quotes)

For example, to display "Pass" in blue for "True" values and "Fail" in red for "False" values, set the Format property to:

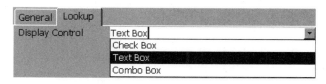

Note: *A custom Yes/No format will not display when used with a checkbox control on a form or report. To change this for the Datasheet view of a table, open the table in Design view and change the Display Control property (on the Lookup tab) to either Text Box or Combo Box.*

149

Add an Input Mask to a Text Box Using a Wizard

The Input Mask property is commonly used to assure that data such as telephone numbers, zip codes, and Social Security numbers are entered correctly and completely.

Notes:

- An input mask will prevent letters from being entered where numbers should be and vice versa. The Input Mask property will also format the display of values stored in a table, much like the Format property. It will, in fact, override the Format property if both are used.

You can set the Input mask by:

Opening table in Design view and selecting the General tab of the Field Properties pane.

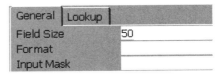

OR

by selecting the Data tab of the property sheet in any other view:

1 Open a form or report in Design view.

2 Select the text box to which you would like to add an input mask.

3 Open the property sheet (see **Open the Property Sheet**).

4 Select the Data tab.

5 Click the Input Mask field on the property sheet:

6 Click the Expression Build button ⬛ to open the Input Mask Wizard.

The following dialog box displays:

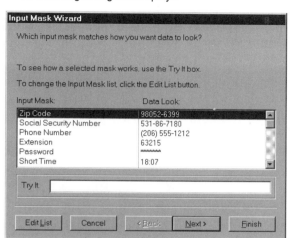

7 Select an input mask from the list:

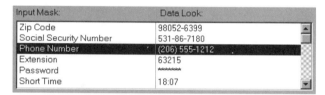

Note: You can also edit existing input masks or create your own by clicking .

8 Type a phone number into the Try It field:

Notice how the mask displays an underscore as a placeholder for each required character as well as additional formatting characters like the parentheses and hyphen used in a phone number. Each underscore is replaced by a character as you type. Formatting characters are skipped over and you'll get a beep if you try to type an invalid character. If you fail to fill in the field entirely, you'll get a message like this:

9 Click  .

10 Change the input mask if desired:

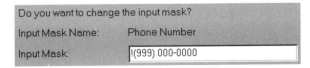

Notes:

• You can select a placeholder from the drop-down list or type your own.

11 Change the placeholder character if desired:

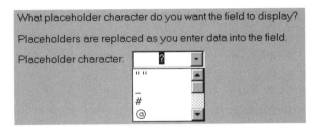

Try it again to see if the changes you made are what you expected:

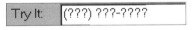

12 Click  .

Decide whether or not you want to store the formatting symbols:

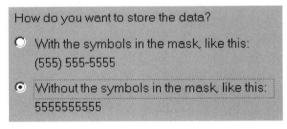

Note: Field size may have to be adjusted if the input mask causes a field to be longer than originally specified.

13 Click  or [Finish] .

The Input Mask property will be filled in appropriately according to the choices you made:

Next Section

Set Default Control Properties

Default control properties determine how new controls will look when added to a form or report. If you want all your fields to be a certain size, with a certain font and color, for example, you can set these properties once, and all subsequently added controls of that type will have the same properties.

Open a form or report in Design view.

Set the Default Control Style

1   Open the property sheet (see **Open the Property Sheet**).

2   Display the Toolbox (see **Toolbox Basics**).

3   Select a control in the Toolbox for which you would like to set the default properties.

The property sheet title bar changes to the word "Default" followed by the name of the currently selected control in the Toolbox. For example, if you select the Text Box control, the property sheet title bar looks like this:

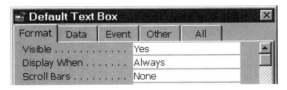

4   Make desired changes to any of the available properties for the currently selected control.

Thereafter, any time you add a control of that type to the current form or report, it will have the same default properties.

Set the Default Control Style to Match an Existing Control

1   Add a control and format as desired.

    OR

    Select a control whose format you'd like to match.

2   Select [Set Control Defaults] from the **Format** menu.

Thereafter, any time you add a control of that type to the current form/report, it will have the same default properties.

Set the Default Control Style for Every Form or Report

Notes:

- To be able to use the same form or report template in all databases, you must copy it to each one. Although Access stores the correct template name on the Forms/Reports tab in the Options dialog box, it will use the Normal template for default properties when the form or report is not in the current database.

1 Format all controls as desired.

2 Save the form or report.

3 Select 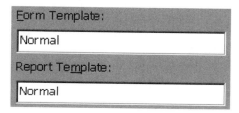 from the **Tools** menu.

4 Select the `Forms/Reports` tab.

5 Enter the name of the form or report you just saved in the appropriate Template field:

> **Form Template:**
>
> Normal
>
> **Report Template:**
>
> Normal

Thereafter, controls added to any new or existing forms or reports will have the default properties you saved in the form or report specified in the Form Template/Report Template.

Enable/Disable/Lock/Unlock a Control

At times it may be necessary to enable/disable certain controls depending on specific conditions. For instance, if your form has a save button, you may want it to be disabled until fields are filled in. It may also be necessary to display data but not allow it to be edited (to open it as read-only). To accomplish this, Access provides the Enabled and Locked properties.

Notes:

- When a control is disabled, it will be dimmed, and you will not be able to either click on it or tab to it. You can leave a control enabled so that it displays normally and you can select it and copy data from it, but to prevent changes to the data, set the Locked property to Yes.

1 Open a form in Design view.

2 Select one or more controls.

3 Open the property sheet (see **Open the Property Sheet**).

4 Select the ⬛ Data ⬛ tab.

Enabled/Disabled

To enable a control, select Yes in the Enabled drop-down list:

An enabled text box looks like this:

Unit Price: $10.00

To disable a control, select No in the Enabled drop-down list:

The same text box, disabled, looks like this:

Unit Price: $10.00

Locked/Unlocked

To lock a control, select Yes in the Locked drop-down list:

To disable a control, select No in the Locked drop-down list:

Locking/Unlocking a control does not affect the way it looks unless the control is also disabled. When a disabled control is locked, it looks just like an enabled control (see above).

156

Next Section

Add a Validation Rule to a Text Box

A validation rule will narrow or restrict the range of values that can be entered into a field or control. For example, a validation rule for a quantity field might check to make sure that a value greater than zero is entered. You could also restrict entries in a date field to be between two dates or greater than after some other date.

Notes:

* A default validation rule can also be entered for a field in the Field Properties pane of a table in Design view. If both a field validation rule and a control validation rule are used, data will be validated against both rules.

1 Open a form in Design view.

2 Select a text box to which you'd like to add a validation rule.

OR

Add a new text box to which you will add a validation rule.

3 Open the property sheet (see **Open the Property Sheet**).

4 Select the | Data | tab.

5 Type the rule against which you'd like to validate your data into the | Validation Rule . . . . . . >=Date() | text box.

OR

Click the Expression Builder button | ... | next to the Validation Rule field to build an expression.

6 Click | OK |.

The validation rule above, for example, ensures that dates are not entered that are earlier than today's date.

7 Into the | Validation Text . . . . . . Date cannot be previous to today. | text box, type the text to display when a value that breaks the validation rule is entered.

Next Section

Create a Macro

Macros can perform one or more actions. Additionally, several related macros can be stored together to create a macro group with one name. Among other things, a macro can display a message, open a form, print a report, run a query, set/remove a filter, or all of the above.

1 Open a database.

2 Select the [🗇 Macros] tab in the Database window.

3 Click [New].

The **Macro** dialog box appears:

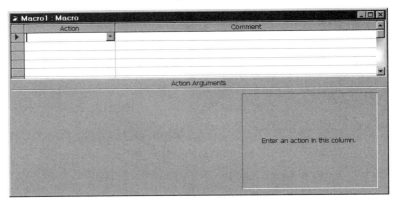

Note: *The macro described in the following steps displays a message box on the screen.*

Notes:

- Each action will have a different set of Action Arguments (bottom pane of the macro dialog box). Press **F1** while in an argument field to get help with the choices.

Notes:

- Up to three lines can be displayed in a message box, each with a blank line between them. Separate the text for each line with the @ symbol. If you only need two lines, you must still include the second @ symbol: Line 1@Line 2@.

Create Message Box Macro

1 Select MsgBox from the Action drop-down list.

2 Enter a Comment, if desired, describing what the action will do.

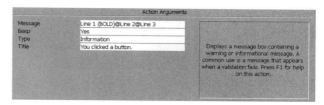

3 Enter a message to be displayed in the message box.

4 Select Yes if you want the message box to beep when it displays.

5 Select what type of icon should be displayed:

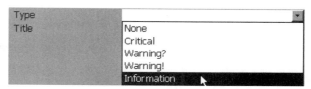

6 Add a title for the message box in the Title field:

Repeat the above procedures for as many actions as you would like the macro to perform.

7 Click the Save button on the toolbar.

8 Type a name for the new macro:

9 Click OK.

Create a Macro Group

Storing macros in groups makes it easier to organize and edit them.

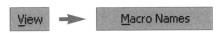

Notes:

- If you have six macros, for example, each attached to a button on a particular form, you could group them and name the macro group FormButtons. In this way, you keep all the related macros for a particular form together and they can all be edited at once without your having to open each one separately.

Notes:

- You may want to rename an existing macro before saving it as a macro group. This way, you can choose a more meaningful name for the group instead of having a name that refers only to one macro.

Notes:

- The names of macros in a macro group are retained even if you choose not to display the Macro Name column.

1 Create a new macro.

OR

Open an existing macro in Design view.

2 Click the Macro Names button on the Macro Design toolbar.

A Macro Name column will display in the Macro window:

Macro Name	Action
	MsgBox

ContinueMsg : Macro

3 Type a name in the Macro Name column.

4 Fill in the Action, Comment (if desired) and Action Arguments fields (see **Create a Macro**).

Repeat the steps above to add macros to the macro group.

5 Click the Save button on the toolbar.

6   If this is a newly created macro, type a name for it:

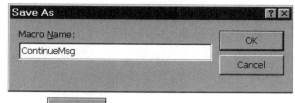

7   Click ⬚ OK ⬚.

163

Attach a Macro to an Event

A macro can be attached to any event on the property sheet. The macro will run whenever the event occurs. For instance, every time you click a command button, the On Click event occurs. By setting the On Click event for the command button to the name of a macro, you make the macro run every time you click that command button.

1   Open a form or report in Design view.

2   Add a command button (see **Add a Command Button to a Form**).

3   Open the property sheet.

4   Select the Event tab:

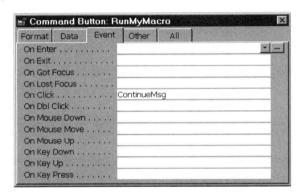

5   Select (or type) the macro name from the drop-down list for the event to which you want to attach the macro. In this example, the macro will be attached to the On Click event so that the macro runs when the command button is clicked:

Macros in a macro group are displayed with a two-part name in the drop-down list, like this:

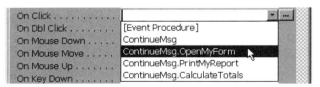

If you select the macro group name instead of a macro defined in the group, the first macro in the group will run.

164

Next Section

Add a Condition to a Macro

When a macro action has a condition, it will only run when the condition is evaluated as True. You can use a condition to do more complex data validation than is possible with the Validation Rule property and display appropriate warnings or messages when necessary.

1 Create a new macro.

OR

Open an existing macro in Design view.

2 Click the Conditions button 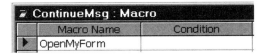 on the Macro Design toolbar.

A Condition column will display in the Macro window:

ContinueMsg : Macro		
	Macro Name	Condition
▶	OpenMyForm	

3 Type an expression into the Condition cell next to the action in the macro that you would like to run conditionally.

The following macro displays a message only if today's date is 12/31/99:

Condition	Action
Date()=#12/31/99#	MsgBox

If there are several consecutive actions in a macro that you would like to run based on a condition, type the condition in the Condition column next to the first action, then type "..." (ellipsis) in the Condition column next to each of the actions that follow that are to be run only if the condition is met.

To run several consecutive actions based on a condition:

- type a condition next to the first action

- type "..." (ellipsis) in the Condition column next to each of the actions that are to be run if the condition is met (these must be consecutive)

When the condition is not met, the action with the condition in the Condition column and each of the actions with "..." in the Condition column will be skipped. The macro will then continue with the next action.

The following macro displays a message if today's date is 12/31/99, then stops. If today's date is not 12/31/99, the macro will start with the OpenForm action, skipping the MsgBox action and the StopMacro action:

Condition	Action
Date()=#12/31/99#	MsgBox
...	StopMacro
	OpenForm

167

Create an AutoKeys Macro Group

When a macro is assigned to a keystroke combination that Access uses, it replaces the default behavior of that keystroke combination.

 Insert → Macro

1 Create a new macro.

2 Click the Macro Names button.

3 Enter a keystroke or keystroke combination in the Macro Name column. The following macro names can be used:

Macro Name	Keys to Press to Run Macro
^a-^z (case insensitive) or ^0-^9	Ctrl + letter or number
{F1} – {F12}	Any function key (F1 – F12)
^{F1} – ^{F12}	Ctrl + Any function key (F1 – F12)
+{F1} – +{F12}	Shift + Any function key (F1 – F12)
{Insert}	Insert (Ins)
^{Insert}	Ctrl + Insert (Ins)
+{Insert}	Shift + Insert (Ins)
{Delete} or {Del}	Delete (Del)
^{Delete} or ^{Del}	Ctrl + Delete (Del)
+{Delete} or +{Del}	Shift + Delete (Del)

4 Select the action(s) you wish this keystroke to perform in the Action column, just as you would with a normal macro. Repeat the previous two steps until you have defined all the keys you want to use.

5 Click the Save button on the toolbar.

6 Type **AutoKeys** as the name for the new macro group:

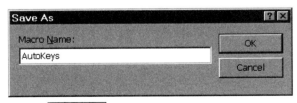

7 Click OK.

Next Section

Special Macro Actions

Echo, SetWarnings, and Hourglass are macro actions that can be used to change what the user sees when a macro runs.

Notes:

- You can use the Echo action more than once in a macro and change the text displayed on the status bar.

Notes:

- With Warnings On set to No, system messages will not be displayed. However, error messages will still be displayed, as will dialog boxes requiring user input.

Notes:

- In Windows 95/Windows NT 4.x, the icon displayed when you use the Hourglass action will be determined by the current setting for Busy. This setting can be found on the Pointers tab in the Mouse Properties dialog box. To change the icon that displays, open the Mouse Properties dialog from the Control Panel folder, select the Pointers tab and choose a different icon for Busy.

Echo

To hide what happens when a macro runs, add an Echo action at or near the beginning.

Set Echo On to No in Action Arguments; optionally, add the text you want displayed in the Status Bar Text field:

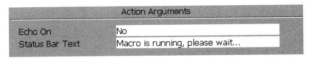

To begin showing what happens in the macro or to change the status bar text, add another Echo action to the macro and set the arguments appropriately.

SetWarnings

To hide system messages while the macro is running, add a SetWarnings action.

Set Warnings On to No in Action Arguments:

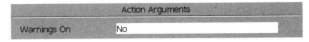

To begin showing system messages later in the macro, add another SetWarnings action and set it to Yes.

Hourglass

To change the mouse pointer to an hourglass while a macro is running, add an Hourglass action.

Set Hourglass On to Yes in Action Arguments:

Action Arguments	
Hourglass On	Yes

To change the mouse pointer back to an arrow, add another Hourglass action and set it to No.

171

Import Data from Another Database

Importing data is much like copying it. Data stored in different formats can be imported into one or more Access tables. The source data is not modified in any way and remains intact.

File → Get External Data ▸ → 🖫 Import...

1 Open a database into which you would like to import data (or objects).

2 In the Database window, select the ⊞ Tables tab, then click New .

3 In the New Table dialog box, double-click on Import Table.

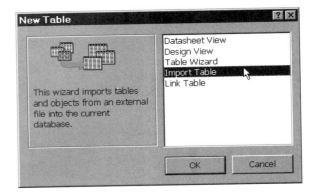

4 The Import dialog box will open. In the **Look In** list box, select the folder which contains the database/table you would like to import.

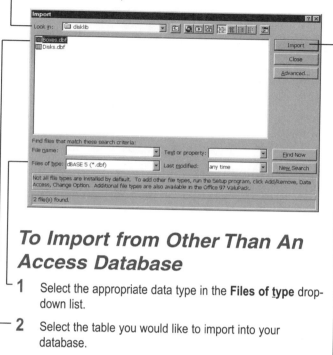

To Import from Other Than An Access Database

1 Select the appropriate data type in the **Files of type** drop-down list.

2 Select the table you would like to import into your database.

3 Click **Import**.

A message box confirms that the table was imported:

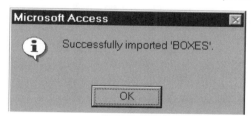

Repeat the steps above to import additional tables, if desired.

4 Click **Close**.

The imported table(s) will be displayed on the Tables tab in the Database window.

To Import from an Access Database

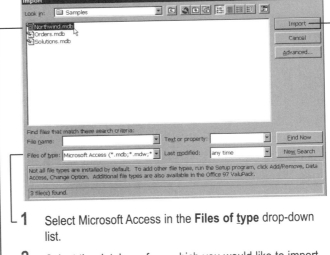

Notes:

- If you choose to import queries, forms, reports, etc., you must also import the associated tables. Otherwise you'll get errors when you try to run them, because the source tables will not be present in the current database.

Notes:

- You can make multiple selections either by clicking or by moving the selector with a cursor key then pressing the space bar.

Notes:

- The Select All/Deselect All buttons only affect the objects on the current tab.

1 Select Microsoft Access in the **Files of type** drop-down list.

2 Select the database from which you would like to import tables or other objects.

3 Click Import.

The Import Objects dialog box will open:

Notes:

- When complete, each imported object will be in the Database window on the appropriate tab.

4 Select the objects you want to import from each tab in the Import Objects dialog box. They will all be processed at once when you click **OK**. The selections you make will be retained as you move back and forth among the tabs in the dialog box.

To select all objects on the current tab, click **Select All**. To deselect all objects on the current tab, click **Deselect All**.

5 Click ⬛ OK when all selections have been made.

The dialog box will show the name of each object as it is imported.

Import Data from a Spreadsheet

Excel data can add supporting documentation to an Access database.

1 Open a database into which you would like to import spreadsheet data.

2 In the Database window, select the ▦ Tables tab, then click New .

3 In the New Table dialog box, double-click on Import Table.

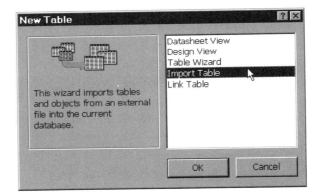

4 The Import dialog box will open. In the **Look in** list box, select the folder which contains the spreadsheet you would like to import.

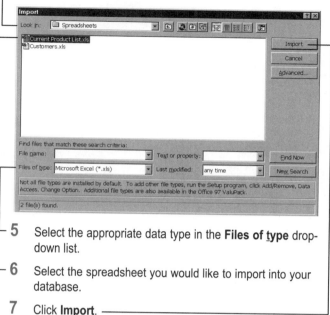

5 Select the appropriate data type in the **Files of type** drop-down list.

6 Select the spreadsheet you would like to import into your database.

7 Click **Import**.

- You cannot control which rows or columns are imported from a spreadsheet using the Import Spreadsheet Wizard. To select only certain rows and/or columns to be imported, open the worksheet, name a range with the rows you want to import into Access, then save the worksheet. When you run the Import Spreadsheet Wizard, choose the **Show Named Ranges** option and select the range you named previously.

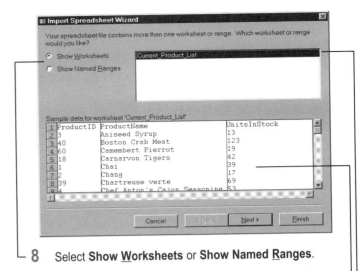

8 Select **Show Worksheets** or **Show Named Ranges**.

If more than one worksheet/range is listed, choose the one you want to import.

A sample of how the Wizard interprets the data is displayed at the bottom.

9 Click **Next >**.

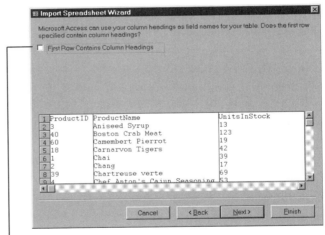

10 Click **First Row Contains Column Headings** if the first row has column headings and not data. The sample shown has column headings in row 1.

11 Click **Next >**.

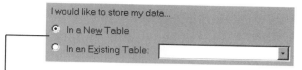

12 Select **In a New Table** or **In an Existing Table**. If you select the latter option, choose the existing table from the drop-down list.

13 Click ![Next >].

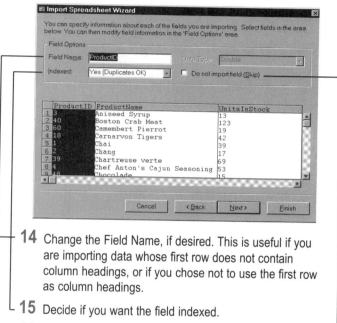

14 Change the Field Name, if desired. This is useful if you are importing data whose first row does not contain column headings, or if you chose not to use the first row as column headings.

15 Decide if you want the field indexed.

16 Check here to skip this field. ———————————

17 Click in each column (field) in the bottom of the dialog box and repeat steps 14-16 above.

18 Click ![Next >].

179

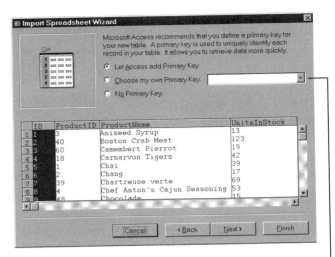

19 Select an option for a Primary Key. The **Choose my own Primary Key** option allows you to select one of the fields being imported as the primary key.

20 Click Next >.

21 Type a name for the new table (if you chose to import into a new table):

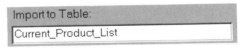

22 Click Finish.

A confirmation message will display:

The new table will be displayed on the Tables tab in the Database window (if you chose to import into a new table).

Next Section

Import Data from a Delimited/Fixed Width File

Delimited and fixed width text files (commonly referred to as ASCII files) are used as a means for importing data when no other format is available or supported.

Notes:

- Delimited and fixed width files typically have extensions like .CSV (comma separated values), .ASC (ASCII), and .TXT (text).

1 Open a database into which you would like to import delimited or fixed width data.

2 In the Database window, select the ⊞ Tables tab then click New .

3 In the New Table dialog box, double-click on Import Table.

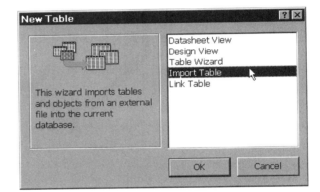

4 The Import dialog box will open. In the **Look in** list box, select the folder which contains the text file you would like to import.

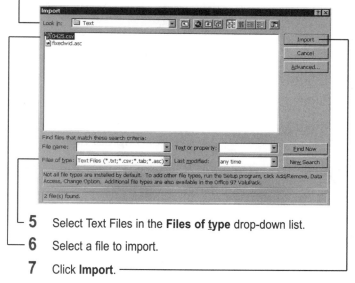

Notes:

• The Wizard is pretty good at determining the correct choices for the delimiter and the text qualifier, but be sure to double-check them on this screen.

5 Select Text Files in the **Files of type** drop-down list.

6 Select a file to import.

7 Click **Import**.

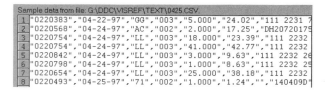

Notes:

• Unless it is done regularly between the same text file and table (or the table is empty), importing data into an existing table is not recommended. It is much easier to re-import data than to clean up a table with data that was imported incorrectly.

8 Select **Delimited** or **Fixed Width**.

The sample window at the bottom of the screen displays several rows from the data file to be imported. Check here if you're not sure if the file is delimited or fixed width.

A delimited file will have some sort of separator (delimiter) between fields, usually a comma, and the data will probably not line up in columns all the way across. Delimited data looks like this:

```
Sample data from file: G:\DDC\VISREF\TEXT\0425.CSV.
1 "0220383","04-22-97","GG","003","5.000","24.02","111 2231 7
2 "0220568","04-24-97","AC","002","2.000","17.25","DH20720175
3 "0220754","04-24-97","LL","003","18.000","23.39","111 2232
4 "0220754","04-24-97","LL","003","41.000","42.77","111 2232
5 "0220842","04-24-97","LL","003","3.000","9.63","111 2232 26
6 "0220798","04-24-97","LL","003","1.000","8.63","111 2232 25
7 "0220654","04-24-97","LL","003","25.000","38.18","111 2232
8 "0220493","04-25-97","71","002","1.000","1.24","","140409D"
```

183

A fixed width file will not have a delimiter and the columns will line up like this:

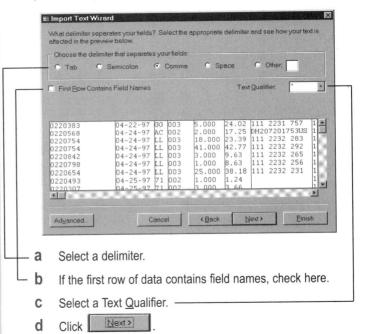

Sample data from file: G:\DDC\VISREF\TEXT\FIXEDWID.ASC.

1	02Z15	1	0.00	0.00
2	02AB17	1	0.00	0.00
3	02AB14	1	0.00	0.00
4	02Z5	1	0.00	0.00
5	020AX2	1	10.00	10.00
6	02AB10	1	25.00	25.00
7	02G6	9	4.50	40.50
8	02N317	2	4.50	9.00

9 Click [Next >].

For Delimited Files

(first complete steps 1-9)

Notes:

- The Text Qualifier is used to surround characters in a field that are to be imported as text. Typically, this is used when the text being imported has the delimiter (like a space or a comma) within a field. By identifying a text qualifier (such as a quote), any delimiter characters between the surrounding text qualifier characters will be imported as part of the field and will not be interpreted as a delimiter. Also, if dates and numbers are surrounded with a text qualifier in the delimited file, they will be imported as text unless you change the data type later in the Wizard.

a Select a delimiter.

b If the first row of data contains field names, check here.

c Select a Text Qualifier.

d Click [Next >].

For Fixed Width Files
(first complete steps 1-9)

If you are importing a fixed width file, this will be the next dialog box displayed:

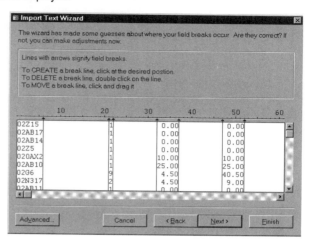

Notes:

- In the example shown, additional field breaks have been added to create blank fields out of the extra space. You can choose not to import these blank fields in a later step. You can also move field breaks by dragging them with the mouse.

a Add field breaks as necessary by clicking in the sample data at the appropriate position.

b Click **Next >**.

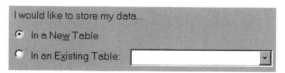

10 Select **In a New Table** or **In an Existing Table**. If you select the latter option, choose the existing table from the drop-down list.

11 Click **Next >**.

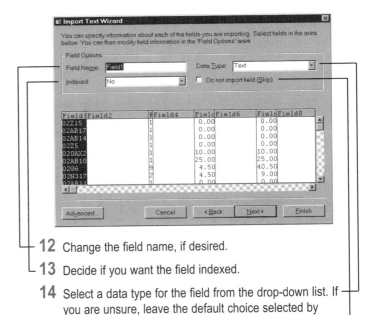

12 Change the field name, if desired.

13 Decide if you want the field indexed.

14 Select a data type for the field from the drop-down list. If you are unsure, leave the default choice selected by Access.

15 Check here to skip this field. In the example shown, Field2, Field4, Field6 and Field8 will be skipped.

16 Click in each column (field) in the bottom of the dialog box and repeat steps 12-15 above.

17 Click [Next >].

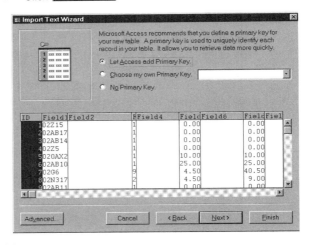

18 Select an option for a Primary Key.

19 Click [Next >].

20 Type a name for the new table (if you chose to import into a new table):

Import to Table:

Fixedwid

21 Click ⌐Finish⌐ .

A confirmation message will display:

Import Spreadsheet Wizard

Finished importing file 'G:\DDC\visref\Spreadsheets\Current Product List.xls' to table 'Current_Product_List'.

OK

Notes:

• If you choose to import into a new table, the new table will be displayed on the Tables tab in the Database window.

Export a Table/Query to a Spreadsheet

The same data stored in an Access table can be used in a spreadsheet without retyping. This is accomplished by exporting.

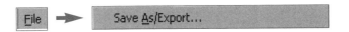

File → **Save As/Export...**

1   Open a database.

2   Select the **Tables** or **Queries** tab.

3   Select a table or query to export.

4   Select **Save As/Export** from the **File** menu.

5   Select **To an External File or Database** in the Save As dialog box:

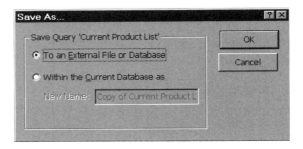

6   Click **OK**.

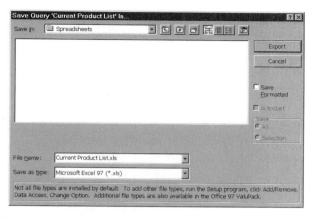

7   Select the folder into which you would like to export the table/query from the **Save in** list box.

8   Select the desired spreadsheet type in the **Save as type** drop-down list.

9   Change the **File name** if desired (the default name is the name of the object being exported).

10 Click [Export] .

To Export a Selection to Microsoft Excel

1   Open a datasheet.

2   Select desired data to be exported.

3   Select **Tools**, **Office Links**, **Analyze it with MS Excel**:

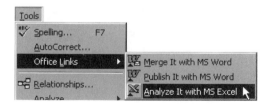

The selected data will be saved in an XLS file in the Access default database folder with the same name as the datasheet. Excel will launch and load that file automatically.

189

If a file with that name already exists, you will get this message:

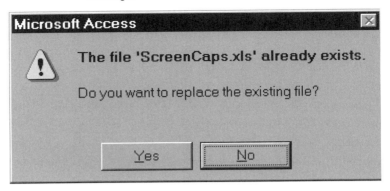

Microsoft Access

⚠ **The file 'ScreenCaps.xls' already exists.**

Do you want to replace the existing file?

| Yes | No |

4 Click Yes to replace the existing file.

OR

If you click No, the following dialog box opens:

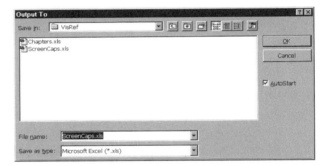

You can change the file name, and/or the folder in which the file will be saved.

5 Click [OK].

Glossary

Action	The basic unit of a macro.
Argument	A variable, expression, or constant that is supplied to a function or action which modifies the result of the function or action.
AutoNumber	Access field type that automatically inserts a sequentially numbered value in each record.
Bound control	A control on a form or report that displays field data stored in an underlying table.
Bound object frame	A control on a form or report that displays a graphic stored in a field in an underlying table.
Calculated control	A control on a form or report that displays the result of an expression rather than data stored in an underlying table.
Calculated field	A field in a query that displays the result of an expression rather than data stored in an underlying table.
Cell	A single rectangle of a datasheet or design grid that can contain data or instructions.
Check box	A control on a form or report that displays a check for a yes/true conditioning or nothing (unchecked) for a no/false condition.
Clipboard	The area of windows memory where any cut or copied information is stored and from which stored information is pasted. The clipboard is automatically overwritten each time a cut or copy operation is performed.
Combo box	A control on a form or report that can display a drop-down list or accept user-typed data.
Command button	A control on a form or report that can be set to run a macro or event procedure when it is clicked.
Concatenation	The adding together of separate text values (strings) for display as one string on a form or report.
Control	Any of a variety of graphical objects on a form or report. A control can be bound, unbound, or calculated, and can take the form of a text box, label, command button, line, rectangle, or picture.
Criteria	Instructions to limit records to be displayed in a query, form, or report.
Data	Information stored in tables in a database.

Datasheet	Data from a table or query displayed in columns and rows (spreadsheet-style).
Design view	The mode in which form or report layouts can be modified.
Embed	To insert a copy of an OLE object created in another application that can continue to be edited in that application.
Event	An action such as a mouse click or keypress recognized by an object.
Export	To copy an object or data to a separate file (usually in another format) that can be used by another application.
Expression	A combination of fields, constants, variables, operands and functions, the result of which is a single value.
Field	One item of information in a record of a table; a column in datasheet view.
Filter	Criteria applied to a group of records to limit the display or printing of records to a subset.
Find	Criteria applied to a group of records to display, one at a time, records meeting the criteria.
Font	The particular design of the letters, numbers, and symbols used to display data.
Footer	A section of a form or report that appears at the bottom of a window or page, or at the end of a report.
Form	An object that contains controls arranged for displaying data on the screen.
Frame	A control on a form or report that can contain an OLE object.
Function	A subprogram used to compute and return a value.
Grid	Data displayed in column and row format, known as a datasheet. Also, a design aid in Design view.
Header	A section of a form or report that appears at the top of a window or page, or at the beginning of a report.
Index	A file in which field values are stored in a sorted order. Indexes speed up searches, queries and filters.
Keyword	A word with a specific meaning in Access that causes predefined events to occur.
Label	An unbound control that displays text on a form or report.
Link	A reference to an object from another application in an Access table, form, or report. The object is stored in the base application.
List box	A control on a form or report that displays a list of values.
Macro	A stored set of actions and their arguments that automate tasks and can be activated through any of a variety of events.

192

Module	Declarations, statements, and procedures that are stored as one unit.
Object	An individual element of an Access database. An object can be a table, query, report, form, or control or text box on a form or report, among other things.
OLE object	An object from an application that supports object linking and embedding.
Operator	A keyword or symbol (e.g., And, Not, +, -, /, *) that indicates the action to be taken usually between two values, strings or variables.
Option button	A control that can be selected or cleared. Almost always part of an option group.
Option group	Several option buttons, only one of which can be selected at any time. Also known as radio buttons.
Orientation	The position of text on a printed page. Either landscape (horizontal) or portrait (vertical).
Parameter	A criterion that can be entered in a query at run time by the user. Also, another word for an argument.
Preview	To view on the screen the printed version of a table, query, form or report.
Primary key	A field (or combination of fields) that uniquely identifies a record.
Property	An attribute of an object.
Property sheet	A list of properties that can be edited.
QBE grid	The bottom part of a query window.
Query	A stored set of instructions regarding displaying or changing data in a table.
Record	One row of data in a table.
Relationship	A link between two fields in one or more tables of a database.
Report	An object that contains controls arranged for printing data.
Row	Data from a single record in a table or query.
Sort	To arrange records of a table or query in either ascending or descending order based on the field values.
SQL	Structured Query Language: used by Access to query the database.
Subform	A form within a form that can display fields from an additional table or query.
Subreport	A report within a report that can display fields from an additional table or query.
Table	The basic structure underlying a relational database. A table contains data organized in rows (records) and columns (fields).

Template	A stored form or report layout that can be used as the basis for new forms and reports.
Text box	A control on a form or report that displays text and can accept text entries.
Toolbox	A group of buttons from which controls are placed on forms and reports.
Toolbar	A varying group of buttons that aids in database activities and provides shortcuts to menu selections.
Unbound control	A control on a form or report having no data source, usually used for displaying informational text.
Unbound object frame	A control on a form or report containing an OLE object from another application.
Variable	A placeholder in an expression that stores changing data.
Wildcards	Characters that can be used in queries and expressions that stand for any of a number of other characters or numbers.
Wizard	A Microsoft tool that automates many database design tasks.
Zoom box	A window that gives a larger view of information in a cell or field.

Appendix

Listed below are the database templates available through the Database Wizard. Each template contains at least one table; most contain more than one. If there is more than one table available, you can select which tables you wish to include. Each table will contain fields for entering information; any or all of these fields may be selected for inclusion in the database. Each template also offers you a variety of styles and backgrounds.

Address Book

Organizes personal and business contacts. Contains fields for title, first and last names, address, phone number(s), fax number, email address, spouse and children's names, birthday, last date contacted, notes, whether or not to send a card, hobbies, nickname, and health issues.

Asset Tracking

Stores important business information about tangible assets and/or employees. There are tables in which you can list asset categories, asset depreciation history, asset maintenance history, status, employee information, department information, and vendor information. Each of these tables contains several fields that allow you to enter information such as ID numbers, descriptions, locations, values, names, etc., as appropriate to that table.

Book Collection

Allows you to list and locate your books by author, title, quotation and/or topic. The available tables are book information, author information, books-authors conjunction table, quotation information, and topics. Each of these tables allows you to input information about a book or its author, such as the ISBN number of the book or the nationality of the author. The available fields depend on the table selected.

Contact Management

Records information about contacts and calls. Contains tables for contact information, call information, and contact identification. The contact information table contains many of the same fields as the address book. The call information table tracks the date, time, and subject of the call and allows you to take notes about the call. The contact information table allows you to assign identification numbers to contacts.

Donations

Contains information about contributor information, pledge information, and donation campaign information. Contributor information includes the name, address, and phone number(s) of donors. Pledge information tells you what amount was pledged, by whom, when it was promised, when it was paid, and the method of payment. Donation campaign information records information about the contribution campaign itself: when it was started, who the chair is, what the fundraising goal is, etc.

Event Management

Event Management is useful for anyone planning a major event, such as a conference or charitable benefit. This template gives you many options as to what information you would like to record. Available tables include event information, event attendee information, event registration information, event type information, information about employees, event pricing information, my company information, payment information, and payment methods.

Expenses

The Expenses template is useful in tracking company expense accounts. It contains tables for information about employees, expense reports, expense details and expense categories. The information about employees table stores the name, address, and phone numbers of employees, along with their hire dates. The expense report information table tells when an expense report was submitted, by whom, which department it was charged to, and when it was paid. The expense details table details the date, amount and description of charges. The expense categories table places expense items into selected categories.

Household Inventory

The Household Inventory template allows you to record information about your possessions for insurance or other purposes. You can list the model number, manufacturer, serial number, and value of items, as well as their date and location of purchase. There is also a field for notes. Items can be put in categories and/or arranged by room. Rooms and categories can be given ID numbers and names.

Inventory Control

Inventory Control allows you to keep track of items in stock and order data. Designed for corporate use, Inventory Control has tables for information about employees, suppliers, shipping, and purchase orders, as well as product information and information about buying and selling inventory. Available fields depend on the tables selected.

Ledger

Tracks information about accounts and transactions. The Ledger template has a table for transaction information that acts like a bankbook, storing information about the date, amount, and type of transaction conducted, and recording account information. There are also tables for recording and classifying account information.

Membership

Stores information about an organization itself, its members, its committees, and dues. The information about members table stores information similar to that found in an address book. Other tables are available to track information about different membership types, methods of payment, committee types and the name, address and ID of the organization. Available fields vary depending on the tables selected.

Music Collection

Like the Book Collection template, the Music Collection template allows you to track information about items you own. You can store information about recording artists, about each recording (CD, LP or cassette) owned, about individual tracks, and about music categories.

Order Entry

The Order Entry template allows you to store information about customers, employees, orders, products, shipments and payments. You can record the date, type, and amount of each purchase in the orders table, and track how it was shipped in the shipping methods table. There are tables that record the names, addresses, and phone numbers of both customers and employees. There is also a table that allows you to store information about your company.

Picture Library

Stores information about photographs. You can record information about the date, place and photographer of each roll of film as well as the date it was developed in the roll of film table. The photographs table allows you to record the filters, exposure, and other techniques used for each shot. The photograph location information table allows you to assign a description and ID to each location.

Recipes

Stores information about recipes and ingredients, and allows you to assign recipes to categories. There is a recipe table that allows you to record information such as the name of the recipe, its nutritional information, what meal it is for, what ingredients it contains, whether or not it is vegetarian, how long it takes to prepare, etc. You can assign IDs to ingredients in the recipe ingredient list, and assign IDs to food categories in the food category information list.

Resource Scheduling

Allows you to manage information about resources, customers, and scheduling. The resource information table records the name and ID of each resource. There are general and detailed resource scheduling tables and a customer information table that is similar to an address book. The resource type information table allows you to assign IDs to resources.

Service Call Management

Helps service providers keep track of their calls. There are tables designed to store information about customers, employees, and payments. The customer information and employee information tables act like address books, while the payment table acts like a register. There is also a table to record the work orders themselves (when they were placed, by whom, etc.) and other tables to record information about the labor and parts required to complete each work order. Available fields vary depending on the tables selected.

Students and Classes

The Students and Classes template is like a record book for teachers. It tracks information about students and their grades, as well as information about instructors and assignments. The student and instructor tables record personal information and IDs, while the class information table stores such information as the name, course number, length and department of the class. The assignment information table records a description of the assignment and the percentage of the final grade that it is worth.

Time and Billing

The Time and Billing template acts like a time clock; it keeps track of employees and their IDs, which projects they worked on, and how many hours they put in on each project. It also records information about the projects themselves and the clients for whom the projects are performed. Tables for expense and payment information are also included. Available fields vary depending on the tables selected.

Video Collection

Like the Book Collection template, the Video Collection helps you keep track of specific possessions. It allows you to assign IDs and descriptions to each video, as well as track information about actors and specific programs. You can also assign types, or categories, to your videos.

198

Wine List

Allows you to record information about your wine collection. The wine list table allows you to record information about each wine, such as its color, price, market value, bottle size, taste, country of origin, region, vintage, vineyard, serving instructions, percent alcohol, etc. The purchase information table records information about date and location of purchase, as well as purchase price and any comments. Another table allows you to assign types, or categories, to the individual wines.

Workout

The Workout database is like a personal trainer! It tracks which exercises you perform, when you started, how often you do them, repetitions and units of weight, etc. There are tables for workout history, workout information, workout details, types of exercises performed, and exercises performed. Using this template, you can assign IDs to workouts and track exercise activity.

Index